To Father Gerard.

In appreciation of an
inspiring retreat.

Oremus pro invicem —

Robert Harvey

CHRISTIANITY IN THE MARKET-PLACE

CHRISTIANITY
IN THE MARKET-PLACE

BY

MICHAEL DE LA BEDOYERE

THE BRUCE PUBLISHING COMPANY
MILWAUKEE

CONTENTS

CHAPTER

I. FACING THE WORLD
PAGE
    i. WHAT MAN TO-DAY WORSHIPS 9
    ii. CHRISTIANITY SHOULD RECOGNISE THE QUALITY OF THIS
        WORSHIP 12
    iii. THE WORLD IS ALSO A SUFFERING WORLD . . 15
    iv. HOW DOES CHRISTIANITY MEET THESE INTENSE EX-
        PERIENCES? 17
    v. THE DARKNESS OF THE WORLD 19
    vi. THE CHURCH'S DIFFICULTIES IN MEETING THE WORLD'S
        NEED 22
    vii. THE CHURCH IS IN THE WORLD, BUT NOT OF IT . 25
    viii. DANGER IN INDEPENDENCE 28
    ix. THIS CHAPTER SUMMED UP 31

II. THE CHRISTIAN RESPONSE
    i. THE WORLD DOES NOT WANT CHRISTIANITY WITHOUT
        DOGMA 33
    ii. THE WORLD IS SHY OF CHRISTIANITY BECAUSE CHRISTIANS
        ARE TOO ORDINARY— 35
    iii. AND TOO EXTRAORDINARY 36
    iv. TWO VIEWS ABOUT GOD 37
    v. THE CATHOLIC DIFFERS FROM OTHERS . . 39
    vi. THE WORLD EXPECTS BELIEF AND BEHAVIOUR TO BE
        CONSISTENT 40
    vii. THE WORLD'S RHYTHM OF EXCITEMENT TO APATHY
        IMITATED BY CHRISTIANS 42
    viii. THE CHRISTIAN RHYTHM SHOULD BE THE OPPOSITE . 44
    ix. CHRISTIAN APATHY TOWARDS TWO CONSTRUCTIVE URGES
        OF OUR DAY 45
    x. THE REASON WHY 47
    xi. CHRISTIAN EXCITEMENT IN TIME OF NATIONAL CRISIS 49
    xii. THIS CHAPTER SUMMED UP 51

III. THE WAY OF "WISDOM"
    i. THAT COURAGE AND SELF-SACRIFICE FOR RELIGION ARE
        NOT ENOUGH FOR THE WORLD . . . 53
    ii. HARDER TO LIVE CHRISTIANITY THAN TO DIE FOR IT . 54
    iii. THE WAY OF WISDOM DEMANDS A CONSTANT EFFORT TO
        JUDGE AS A CHRISTIAN 58
    iv. THE CHURCH'S COMMISSION IS LIMITED, BUT NOT THE
        INDIVIDUAL CHRISTIAN'S 62
    v. GOD PROVIDES A "SHORT-CUT" TO SALVATION, BUT IT
        DOES NOT WORK FOR SOCIETY AS A WHOLE . 63
    vi. THE "SHORT-CUT" DOES NOT IMPRESS A WORLD WHICH
        HAS LOST FAITH IN DOGMA 65

CHAPTER   PAGE

  vii. THE RESPONSIBILITY IS ON INDIVIDUAL CHRISTIANS, NOT
    THE CHURCH 67
  viii. AN EXAMPLE TAKEN FROM CHRISTIAN PACIFISTS . . 69
  ix. CHRISTIANS AND THE JUSTICE OF WAR . . 72
  x. THIS CHAPTER SUMMED UP . . . 74

IV. THE CHURCH IN ACTION AND WHAT SHE IS FACING

  i. THE CHURCH PRESENTS A FINE PICTURE . . 75
  ii. BUT STILL IT IS OBVIOUSLY NOT ENOUGH—REASONS WHY 76
  iii. THE EXAMPLES OF CATHOLICS IN FRANCE . . 78
  iv. THE CASE OF THE LATIN COUNTRIES . . 78
  v. IN ANGLO-SAXON COUNTRIES . . 81
  vi. IS QUALITY SACRIFICED TO QUANTITY AND SAFETY? 84
  vii. CHARACTERISTICS OF THE REVOLUTION AROUND US—
    GERMANY 86
  viii. THE INEVITABLE CONSEQUENCES ON EUROPE . 87
  ix. THE NATURE OF THE CONTROL TO BE EXERCISED BY THE
    VICTORS 90
  x. AN UGLY PICTURE WE MUST FACE . . 92
  xi. THE RÔLE OF RELIGION . . . 94
  xii. CHRISTIANITY'S REAL TASK . . . 96

V. SOME PRACTICAL POINTS OF REFORM

  i. QUALIFICATIONS FOR MAKING CERTAIN SUGGESTIONS . 97
  ii. EDUCATION 100
  iii. THE PARISH AND THE FAMILY . . 103
  iv. CATHOLIC ORGANISATION THROUGHOUT THE COUNTRY 106
  v. CO-OPERATION BETWEEN CATHOLICS AND NON-CATHOLICS
    —A NEW WAY 109
  vi. THE EFFECT OF INTERNATIONAL CHRISTIAN ACTION
    (SECULAR AS WELL AS RELIGIOUS) ON THE WORLD 117

VI. A NEW PENTECOST

  i. THE REAL DANGER WILL BE IN THE FALSE RECONSTRUC-
    TION AFTER THE WAR . . . 120
  ii. THREE REASONS WHY CHRISTIANITY IS NOT ASKED TO
    HELP 124
  iii. THE LANGUAGE OF CHRISTIANITY IN THE MARKET-PLACE . 128
  iv. A STRUGGLE AGAINST THE STREAM . . 130
  v. THE LINK BETWEEN CHURCH AND WORLD IS THE
    INDIVIDUAL CHRISTIAN DE-MONSTRATING CHRIST . 133
  vi. THE GIFT OF TONGUES WITH WHICH TO SPEAK TO THE
    WORLD 135

INTRODUCTION

In these pages I have tried to face the problem of Christianity's practical failure to impress the contemporary world. It is of course an old question, but Christianity did once convert a pagan empire and mould a new civilisation. Though very many individuals still accept the teachings of Christianity (in varying degrees) for what they call their religious or spiritual life, even *they* have become increasingly "post-Christian"—to use a convenient expression whose meaning is obvious, but which avoids the often inaccurate implications of words like "materialist," "pagan," etc.—in their public, professional, and business lives. Yet if ever there was a time when events testified to the shortcomings of this "post-Christianity," and when the doctrine, traditions, and moral guidance of Christianity seemed (on paper) to be worth serious study, it is to-day. But there appears to be a missing link or something standing between the world and Christianity that prevents the needed connection, some hidden source of constant misunderstandings.

I do not, of course, pretend in this short book to have explored the whole subject, but I believe that I have put my finger on to one of its aspects and one which, as far as I am aware, has not been treated elsewhere. My treatment may be considered superficial by theologians and historians, but I would suggest that one is apt in these deep, yet tremendously important, subjects to become bogged in analysis and theory, and that more light may after all be thrown on to them by a cruder and bolder method. My picture is blocked out roughly and perhaps even coarsely, but the contrast that emerges may be the means of demonstrating the more easily the nature both of the present misfits and of the reshaping that requires to be done if Christianity is to convert a pagan empire for the second time, and to lay once again the foundations of a new order.

This book may be read as a sequel to a previous essay of mine, called *Christian Crisis*,[1] and published at the end of the first year of the War. These pages stand however completely on their own. I write as a Catholic in communion with the See of Rome, and what I say is primarily addressed to my fellow-Catholics. I hope however that it will reach that much wider audience that I have had all the time in mind. I think it is a mistake for a person with certain convictions to attempt to conceal those convictions because he would like to be listened to by others who do not share them and may not always understand their full grounds. My convictions are, in any case, shared by about three hundred million other Christians and, whatever may be thought of them, they are evidently a very important part of the matter that has to be taken into account by those who, from other standpoints, share my hope that Christianity may again leaven a torn and bleeding world. It is then more honest and, I hope, more useful for me to stand fair and square on my own platform and to speak from it. I am all the more indebted to my publisher, Mr Andrew Dakers, who shares my wider hopes while being far from sharing my Catholic convictions, for being willing to take these pages under his protection and offering them to the public. I must also thank Miss C. Galvin, who in this and other work has taken upon herself the thankless task of turning the grindstone and keeping my nose to it.

[1] *Christian Crisis*, by Michael de la Bedoyere (Burns, Oates & Washbourne).

CHAPTER I

FACING THE WORLD

(i) WHAT MAN TO-DAY WORSHIPS

WHAT sort of appeal is Christianity making to-day to the man-in-the-street? That question must be asked and answered in a more candid way than is customary, if the Church is to prove in practice one of the constructive factors in a new world. Let us remember that man has substantially lost his religious faith, as Christians understand it. He may or may not believe in God, but even when he thinks himself to believe in God, his is at best a belief that the universe has some plan and meaning; that there is more in it than meets the eye; that the best thinkers have given up crude materialism; that you cannot explain away the finer things of life without invoking something greater than man; that somehow, somewhere, good will prevail. Quite disconnected with this vague framework of a religious faith, there is generally in contemporary man a very strong moral and intellectual earnestness, which results from intimate association with his fellow-men in some group, such as nation or class or society. Man—I mean of course the non-exceptional man of the Western world—has ceased altogether to *worship* the God of Christianity, even if he does not actually deny His existence, but he is all the time worshipping. In time of war many men worship their country's cause, not so much because it concerns their country, but because their country stands for a moral right, for a decent ideal, for a new order, for a better world. In times of peace the object of this worship is vaguer and more diffused, expressing itself perhaps in an urge towards a social or humanitarian reform,

1*

though for many years the failure of such reform to mature has induced a fanaticism for national or class mass-action.

It is all-important to realise the strength and ubiquity of this modern craving for finding new objects to worship. One may put it this way. So long as men retained a living faith in God and the teaching and values of an established religion, they took themselves and their own personal or social interests with a grain of salt. You cannot really believe in the truths of Christianity and at the same time take an overwhelming interest (worship) in causes and changes so evidently bound up with the short span of human life on earth. I do not mean to say that a general religious belief in the ages of Faith turned men as a whole into mystics who scarcely saw the earth at all, or into cynics who, knowing that the earth did not count for much and feeling themselves somewhat weak in their vision of heaven, took everything with rather more than *one* grain of salt. Men of course loved and fought and sacrificed themselves for their passions and ideals as they do to-day. But under such conditions of religious belief *reason* was always something of a damper. If a man stopped to think, he tended to ask himself: was it worth it? Idealism was either religious or it was a personal passion. Many an evil, it is only too true, was committed in the name of religion, but for a long time the fundamental unity of belief restricted the scope of religious causes and kept men united as to the greater part of their lives and work. Civilisation was one, and men were agreed about the things that mattered and that were worth pursuing. And since men were agreed about this, what mattered was taken for granted and, so to say, did not seem to matter so very much. That is to say, there was no need to be always moralising about the least quarrel or difference. On the other hand, the idealism in pursuit of passion was essentially individual and not social. Men were jealous, lost their tempers, pursued wealth and power, even began social rebellions, and on behalf of these things gladly lost their lives—which is, after all, the best test of real worship—but these causes did not unite great bodies of men into a social or national movement whose size and importance could dwarf God and other-worldly religion. Reason built on religious faith always remained on guard to warn people that, in terms of truth, they were in danger of making mighty fools of themselves. In fact accepted religious belief tended to cause men to underrate rather than to exaggerate the importance of moral and personal causes, and the charge is rightly made that many an injustice crying to Heaven for vengeance was often tolerated because Heaven itself seemed too close to make it worth men's while to bother.

But with the general loss of an agreed religious belief, we have gone to the opposite extreme. Men render to man, to man's works, to man's feelings, to man's judgment and conscience, the worship they once gave to God. The pursuit of social and humanitarian ideals, on the one side, and the revulsion against evils, such as cruelty, aggression, bad faith, on the other, have become so strong that men will gladly destroy half the world because of them. The worship of a better world, according to one's own convictions about a better world, will lead not only to incredible self-sacrifice but to ruthlessness, cruelty, and bitterness unknown on such a scale in past times. Rather than compromise with bad faith, a nation will gladly bleed to death and leave anarchy in its train. And since these moral and idealistic convictions are not based upon an agreed objective truth or order, and since human ignorance makes it inevitable that we act upon an insufficiently informed judgment, we find the world divided, not only into good and bad men, but good and good men, all half-blind and all inflicting cruelties upon one another and denouncing one another as barbarians. Furthermore, since these moral convictions are the product of a common loss rather than of individual passion, they are shared by millions who stand together in their defence. And this evil is made infinitely worse because the technique of modern life plays into the hands of the mass social unit and renders the individual powerless. Reason, so far from acting as a damper on the worship of these ideals, encourages that worship, for apart from them what is left? What kind of a world would be left us, divorced on the one side from a supernatural faith in God, an ideal order laid up in Heaven and the promise of another life, and divorced on the other from these passionate convictions in progress, love, moral uprightness, a new and better order here on earth? Man must worship, must strive, must build, must have an ideal, otherwise he falls to pieces and disintegrates. War itself is welcomed as the means of re-creating the morale of an effete and self-satisfied people, and during war there are many who wonder what will happen after war when men will be deprived of the stimulus of a patriotic and moral cause.

(ii) CHRISTIANITY SHOULD RECOGNISE THE QUALITY OF THIS WORSHIP

Clearly if there was something insufficient about a faith in another world that left men cynical and indifferent about the state of human affairs here below, there is something far more disastrous about a faith in human judgment and human feelings so intense that men will hate and destroy one another and their heritage built up through the centuries in worship of that faith.

To realise this need for worship, and the character of the objects and mode of worship, when the worship of God is no longer real, is to understand where the truth of Christianity should, so to speak, be inserted into the contemporary world. *If you wish to convince a man of the error of*

his ways, you must deal with him where he is strongest, not where
he is weakest. You must show him to be most wrong where
he believes himself to be strongest and most right. There
are many weak points in all of us, and they are all very
vulnerable. To be convinced at that level gets us nowhere.
Preaching of that kind is preaching to the already converted
or to those who will never be interested in conversion.
And Christianity is very apt to attack the world where it is
weakest, not where it is strongest. As a consequence the
world which feels strongly about its faith and the good it
is trying to do despises a Christianity which confines itself
to condemnation of what is obviously weak or evil and
which manifests apparent indifference to this world's most
generous and sincere impulses.

An intelligent man will not easily be converted to a new
faith by a priest who dilates upon the decadence and dis-
soluteness of the times or of the man's personal character,
even though he may very easily be convinced of the truth
of what the priest says. He instinctively feels that it is the
effects and not the causes which are being attacked. And
unless he already shares the priest's faith, he feels that they
are getting nowhere. But convince a man that he is most
wrong and most unreasonable where he believes himself
to be most right and even most virtuous, and then he may
be startled into the realisation that his whole position is
untenable. But to do this successfully the strength and
goodness and idealism of the modern world and of contemporary man must be studied and sympathetically
recognised, for it is in terms of that strength and goodness
and idealism, not of the weakness and decadence and sin,
that the Christian appeal must be made. Contemporary
man is not bad—there is a very real sense in which he is too
much of an idealist. That is patent if we consider the
energy, work, good-will, and skill that have been given to
the cause of peace, of social progress, of education, of

alleviation of suffering, of knowledge, of justice in every respect. Modern man has long been intent on thinking out an acceptable philosophy of life, a way of rationally integrating the different powers within him, of giving to his own and to the life of his fellows a meaning worth the name. And all this earnestness is not confined to the academy or the study. It has been steadfastly pursued in every class and every walk of life. Nor is it purely theoretical. It has prompted a degree and range of devotion that is often heroic. If we read, for example, the testimony of a Bolshevik agent who calls himself John Valtin in *Out of the Night* we find ourselves faced with a series of actions on behalf of an ideal which are only comparable with the annals of the great Christian missionaries and martyrs. That book tells the annals of the modern martyrs, the martyrs in the service of desperate modern ideals. Valtin is no saint, quite apart from the wrongness of his cause. He is dissipated, sexually indulgent, given to every human weakness like so many others—like our contemporary society. Despite this, however, he will endure every discomfort, every danger, every humiliation, every torture in the service of the cause—again, like our contemporary society.

In Russia and Germany thousands have lived as Valtin lived. And greater numbers have heroically suffered in concentration camps and worse for their ideals. And to go no further than this country, what heroism and endurance and charity and patience have been evoked by the consciousness of the nation's peril in a just cause!

For the Christian to dismiss a world like this as just decadent and corrupt is sheer idiocy. The world in return instinctively despises the Church as weak, complacent, and superficial. If we could tabulate the amount of heroism, endurance, self-sacrifice, and charity which faith in the Christian religion has evoked during the last twenty years and compare it with the conduct evoked by faith in these this-world ideals we might at last be startled into a somewhat less complacent frame of mind.

We must face the fact that, questions of rightness and wrongness and therefore of ultimate goodness apart, a Christianity that seems to the world weak and flabby faces a world that appeals as strong and virile. And no amount of proof that Christians say their prayers and practise chastity, while the world gives itself to wine, women, and song, is going to change this fact, nor the underlying consciousness of it in the mind of the world. Indeed the evidence is so strong that an outsider may reasonably ask whether the Christian believes in and worships God to-day in any sense comparable with the way in which the fanatic of the world worships his ideals of a new order or a better world or whatever it may be. By their fruits you shall know them. There is the real problem, and so long as Christians evade it, so long will they be passed over.

(iii) THE WORLD IS ALSO A SUFFERING WORLD

And a similar contrast may be reached from another point of view. The world to-day is a world of suffering, as well as of pleasure. Not only has the clash of faiths given rise to an immensity of suffering, but the very experiments in creating a better world have left behind their wreckage, their trail of suffering. The very failures have left wide gaps open, gaps into which the selfish and the powerful have poured in to take personal advantage of the mistakes made. Furthermore the abyss between the world's idealism and the little it has accomplished has increased the suffering, for men have been led to great expectations and then been thrown on to the roadside as so much useless lumber. In days when men did not expect so much of life, nor worry their heads so persistently to

find the formula which would solve the miseries of the
world, they had time to attend to the individual person.
Their lives were lived in terms of human persons and not
of abstract and, too often, inhuman ideas and theories.
And their belief in God, who was Father and Brother to
men, short-circuited, as it were, blue-prints to perfection.
Men were more content to love and help their brother in
distress for God's sake and not for the sake of a more
perfect world.   And they were not so interested in results.
Love and charity were their own reward.   They were not
so scandalised by the thought of the beggar getting drunk
on the alms he received, because they did not feel that
another beautiful theory for a better world was being
wrecked.   They were content to leave it to God.   To-day
their earthly horizon is unbounded and therefore their
painful disappointments continual.

Men are enduring this mighty tide of suffering, suffering
in social insecurity, in unemployment, in housing that has
neither the human comforts of the bad old days nor the
utility promised for to-morrow, in wages often lower than
ever in relation to the show and glamour of the advertised
life of the day, in serfdom as the cog in the machines of
industry and State, in the loss of a simple faith that comforts
and sustains, in the appalling horrors—killing, maiming,
exile, and uprooting—imposed by the totalitarian ambitions
of war and the plannings of peace.   And suffering, though
it makes a man bitter, deepens and strengthens his character.
The man who has suffered, who has *seen* things, is a man
who has learnt to think for himself, to judge by basic
human standards, to see through shoddiness and hypocrisy;
he is a man who does not mind suffering a little more if he
begins to see his way to something really promising at last.
Such a man is not going to be convinced by anything that
does not enter into the very marrow of his being.

(iv) HOW DOES CHRISTIANITY MEET THESE INTENSE EXPERIENCES?

In the face of this suffering (which Christians themselves share as men of the world rather than as members of the Church) what is the Church offering? Prayers, sermons, a mumbled, lip-served creed, bourgeois smugness, intolerable self-satisfaction? But that is too often how it looks to those who have *lived*! Dare a Church that preaches Christ Crucified, that teaches the value of suffering, offer to a profoundly suffering world anything less than what the world has suffered! Does the Church, do the Christians, do the clergy themselves make contact with the world at the level of the world's suffering, or do they stand above, hanging on to the last ridges of a world that is gone, away from the dirt and smell and blood, beckoning to those below and expecting them to rise by spiritual enchantment? A Church—a Christian—that gives that impression will not be respected or even heard.

And let us not imagine that, whether it be the world of men working and fighting for the causes they worship or the world of men left to suffer amid the wreckage of those causes, there is anywhere intellectual satisfaction, a sense of security, a realisation that the clue to existence has been found. The frantic struggle to get something done, to work out a plan, to try this or that, to crush those who object, betokens doubt eating away at the roots of the faith. Men cling desperately to nation or Nazism or Bolshevism or whatever it be, because it is all that is left to them. It is that or chaos. Worship is strong, stronger than ever, but only because it is worship with the strung-up nerves, with the alternative of despair. And if this sense of frustration and despair is strong among the leaders, the lucky ones, how much stronger must it be among the victims, the victims who are already delivered to that chaos which keeps their "betters" going!

What face, what appearance, does the Church of God present to this generation trying to save itself by hanging on with numbed grip to this raft or that, or swimming for life in a dark sea? Indeed it may ask where is the one Church of God, where can they find the one explanation that is so often talked about. *He* is a Christian and *he* is a Christian and *he* is a Christian, they will be told. Will they not answer: I see an Englishman in *him*; I see a Nazi in *him*; I see a wealthy business man in *him*; I see a good administrator deeply preoccupied with the finances of a parish in *him*; I see a dispenser of some magic charm which I cannot understand in *him*; I see a war-monger in *him*; I see an echo of this or that national or class or social propaganda in *him*; I see a skilful diplomat who tells me that all will come right in *him*, and I very often see all the signs of a gentleman in *him* and *him* and *him*—but I have yet to discover in any of these that inspiration, that fire, that light, that order, which can attract me and warm me and guide me away from all these divisions, fanaticisms, conflicts that tear me to pieces, that better world of which men speak, that Christianity. Rather do I find in one after the other some aspect, some effect of the universal madness, and in them I find it coolly and politely and sensibly formulated in terms of some complex philosophy studied in a comfort and security of mind and body which I shall never know. Whatever the secret may be, it is apparently well hidden away, and its effect would not seem to be to cause a man or a people to be reborn, but to give him the power to behave exactly as everyone else does without soiling his soul. The Christian pats me on the back, calls me by my first name, leaves me to do the dirty work and then condemns me. Given my particular position and my particular needs, it does not seem so very enticing.

(v) THE DARKNESS OF THE WORLD

I have drawn a grim picture and an unfair picture: a caricature. And I have not suggested that this is the Church; I have suggested that this is how many see the Church. But it is in caricatures that we catch an aspect of a person that has been hidden from us, his best friends. I have drawn a distorted picture of a Church that is only interested in the weaknesses, the decadence of the world, not recognising its virility and its heroisms, its faiths and its ideals, and not realising that it is only by meeting the world on that strong, that real, ground that it can hope to impress the world; a Church that does not recognise the suffering in the world and does not itself suffer as a Church; a Church that, instead of fearlessly offering to the world a message of salvation practised and lived in its members, appears before the world in the persons of those who represent it divided, as other men are divided, dispensing not the seeds of new life, but a prophylactic enabling a man and the world to continue as they are, hiding the Jacob's ladder pitched between Heaven and Charing Cross.

To avoid misunderstanding, let me make it clear that I am not suggesting that the contemporary world is to be admired. My point is that the world presents a picture of heroism, good-will, and suffering, but in disorder and in increasing corruption. By contrast the Church may seem to be proposing an attractive order on paper, but doing so complacently, half-heartedly—at a level of experience that is much shallower than that of the world. The individual Christian will not suffer for his religious ideals a tenth of what he is prepared to suffer for his country or his political cause, while the Church itself appears too often to be content to chide the world for its sins without seeking to interpenetrate the world, understand its motives and feelings in the surrounding darkness, and convert the world by that "suffering with," that deep understanding which alone can form a strong bridge between the world and the Church, between man and God.

Catholics know perfectly well that even if the picture which I have drawn were not a caricature—a caricature in that much of the truth is distorted and omitted, and a caricature in that the scale on which the picture is drawn is out of proportion to the very meaning and aims of Christianity—the truth of it would still not affect in the slightest the claims of the Church to be Divine. But we are here dealing, not with the nature and teaching of the Church in itself, but with the actual picture of the Church to-day in relation with the modern world. Both from the side of the world and from the side of the Church there exists a desperate demand that the one should come to understand the other better, for the world to-day is being destroyed under our eyes and has not yet tried Christianity, and the Church knows that one thing only can save the world and that is the restoration of belief in God and the pattern of life which God has revealed. Indeed to the Christian it is painfully simple to see the defects of the world and of its plans. No ideology has yet been offered which does not carry plain evidence of the bad in it and the good; no blue-print that does not fail because it leaves out man as Christianity knows him to be. We must therefore seek at all costs—not least to our own pride—to find the way to bridge the abyss between world and Church. And by far the heavier duty falls upon the Church, for the reason why the world needs Christianity so insistently is because the world is more blind than evil. But if the world sees the Church as I have sought to picture it, what hope is there of the two meeting again?

I repeat that I do not believe the world to-day to be as evil as many Christians seem to contend. I do not even

believe the world to be as evil as it often thinks itself.
There is of course immense evil in the world, but it is very
definitely the Devil's evil: the evil of ignorance and blind-
ness and pride, of which men can only be made conscious
by God's help. Conscious evil, the evil of envy, of greed,
of covetousness, of selfishness, of the lust for power, above
all, of those many sins of omission which result from
egotism and the search for comfort, luxury, money, show,
and ever-keener refinements of pleasure, these are shared
too often by 'good' Christians. But the world has always
been filled with sin, and I think that sin is preserved by the
Devil, as it were, in a great reservoir and that as channels
of ignorance and pride are formed in the world so does
sin fill them up. Let the earth be in some degree levelled
and order restored, and so will sin tend to dry up. It is
ignorance, pride, and the disorder they cause that produce
the great evils of our time. The cause of the world's
disruption is not to be found in the amount of the sin
against which the preacher inveighs; that is more an effect
than a cause. The cause is to be sought in the darkness
of the mind which is no longer illuminated by the light of
the Holy Spirit. It is because of this darkness that men
plunge forward, often with the courage and heroism of
despair, in pursuit of the good as they obscurely see it,
hating and denouncing their enemy who may be equally
seeking for a partial, veiled good. It is very literally in
the service of the Devil, the Prince of Darkness, that good
men, often the best of men by nature and disposition and
character-training, follow trails artfully mixed and mingled
through past errors. And too often, in the pursuit of
these contrary and contradictory phantoms, they find
themselves attacked and degraded by the evil consequences
even to their own characters of the disorder, the unreason,
the fanatic passion that characterise these godless courses.
So reckless do they become that their conscience is finally

blunted even to the simplest distinction between right and wrong, good and evil. Every and any means to the end is justified. The whole being is coarsened by the hatred, the passion, the vindictiveness with which their cause is worshipped. Common sense is forgotten. Ordinary prudence in weighing one value against the consequences of the loss of another is thrown aside. On the large scale, and perhaps in more outwardly polite terms, nations and peoples treat one another like drunkards, who never feel more virtuous, more certainly in the right, more indignant about the other fellow and ready to denounce him as the Devil, than when liquor begins to obscure the reason and allow free rein to the lower passions. Such, I contend, is the character of the world's evil to-day, and one can but smile to see men of a world which yesterday thought evil out-dated, except as a disease, to-day denouncing and fighting one another over it as though it were as absolute and as powerful as God. Satan indeed can rub his hands with glee as he watches, not the inevitable decay of what is already rotten, but the corruption of the best.

(vi) THE CHURCH'S DIFFICULTIES IN MEETING THE WORLD'S NEED

Naturally, at any given time, there are very different degrees of this evil which springs from the obscuring of God's light. One nation (or party or faction) perhaps with the justest original grievance comes to worship and nurse that grievance so that a veritable mass-hypnosis is developed, and all proportion between the end and the means is lost. Or a genuine grievance is turned by positively evil and self-seeking men into the instrument of their craving for power, wealth, adventure. As against the aggression of such dangerous people, others may be forced to defend themselves, but unfortunately, in a world that has lost any conviction about the true pattern and meaning of life and the real scale of values, self-defence itself can become converted into the pursuit of ends scarcely less limited and one-sided than that of the enemy, while opposition itself to evil soils scarcely less than alliance with it, for both sides find their roots at bottom in the same false values. And underlying all this, and closely resulting from it, there is the social, family, and personal disruption that leads to moral instability, irresponsibility, dishonesty, lawlessness, adolescent crime, the serving of the selfish and lower passions.

It would be very much easier if Christianity could, as it were, condemn the whole world root and branch, stand away from it, preach the truth, and wait for men to recover their sanity. Such has in fact been the method sometimes adopted by forms of religious revivalism. It is however un-Christian, first because it is a false method, and second because it is stupid and impracticable. Good and evil are inextricably confused in the world, as we have seen, and the Christian fidelity to truth lays upon the Church the duty of trying to trace the good, to support it, to bring it back to the right path, to harmonise it again with other goods, to reintegrate it into *the* Good. The Church cannot just condemn all belligerents at the present time; she cannot even totally condemn Germany as her enemies condemn her. For there is good in everything, the good, in fact, whence also conversion can at length come.

That good cannot be condemned by Christianity without Christianity destroying the foundation upon which it must build. On the contrary, it must be freed and strengthened.

But even more important is the Church's realism. The Church was not instituted by Christ to replace the State, even the bad State. Her task is to teach man and States the right path, the pattern which they should follow in pursuing their business. The world cannot suddenly stop, be converted, and start again; it must go on, and every revolution, even a Christian one, only marks a more or less rapid reorientation in values. So far from standing away from the world, and uttering wholesale condemnations of a world that must anyhow go on, the Church's task is to plunge into the fray, into the disorder, into the dirt and squalor, at work all the time on the endless task of setting a better example, counselling, encouraging, helping, and, above all, bringing Christ to sinners and fools.

And we can see that at any given moment *that* in fact is the way in which the Church wants to work. The very actions that scandalise the world find their real explanation in this attempt, too often unsuccessful, to be in the world without being of it.

If Christians are divided into citizens of different countries, if they belong to different factions, if they are to be found in different stations and classes, it is because their Christian apostolate bids them be intimate with every kind of person, every ideal, in the world, be one with them, sharing the sufferings, the joys, the hopes, the aims—in so far as they are good—of each. If the Church does not enter by the world's door, it will never enter at all.

And sometimes non-Christians, or even Christians, are troubled by the patience shown by the Pope and rulers of the Church in dealing with civil governments and parties whom others hastily judge to be beyond redemption. This patience would seem at times to amount to compromise —compromise with the Devil, as the world which does not believe in the Devil, calls it. But the need to be always there and everywhere, disentangling good from evil, is in the mind of the Church, the realisation that the world must go on—that it is rarely as bad as enemies imagine, rarely as good as friends proclaim. The Church, imitating her Master who went with publicans and sinners, tries to fulfil, to better—not to destroy. The point is whether Christians succeed in living up to this difficult ideal.

(vii) THE CHURCH IS IN THE WORLD, BUT NOT OF IT

It is not indeed the easy way; it is by far the hardest. It is a way beset by dangers and pitfalls, for it demands a living and constant detachment of spirit, or the world will judge rightly that Christians in the world, so far from renewing the world, have been caught and bought by it. When the Christian is an Englishman or a Frenchman or a German, sharing all that is good and God-intended in these national differences—these specialities that enhance and enrich the ever-diversified and ever-changing creation of God—he suffers from the constant temptation of putting country and country's cause before the true order of life, of working out a pattern which cannot fit in with the true pattern. It would be so much easier for him to stand away and try to live in a rarefied spiritual realm. But as a Christian he cannot. He is body and soul. He is a human being. He is a citizen of a country. He is a man of business. He is a politician. For the Christian to try to cut himself off from worldly attachments is tantamount to condemning them. But they are the matter which Christianity "informs," and the life of the Christian is not a separated life; it is an ordinary life of the world, but one that fits into God's pattern. Nothing is condemned except disorder, which is a rent in the pattern, or the attempt to make a new pattern that cannot be harmonised with the true design. To be constantly in the world, sharing the world, and yet to be constantly against the ways and values of a world that is seeking the wrong end is the most difficult of ideals, and it would indeed be a miracle if even the best of Christians did not often fail to stand by their ideal.

And that is why it is so easy for the world to condemn the Church, as we have seen it condemned. Much of the caricature which I drew can be better understood in the light of this, the mission of the Church, and the inevitable difficulty of its accomplishment.

Because the Church is intimately mingled with the world —because in a sense it is the world itself in its true moral and spiritual aspect—it is natural enough that the Church should concentrate on the weaknesses rather than the strength of the world. The weakness, the obvious sin, the clear breach of the commandments, these constitute a clear and simple issue. There is no ignorance and confusion on either side. The Church's teaching in the matter of sex, for example, is clear and rigid and, above all, unchanged in theory and application from the beginning. Ever since the beginning the temptations of the flesh have been strong and incessant in fallen human nature. Only comparatively recently has the world tried to rationalise sin in this department in respect of divorce, birth-control, and self-indulgence outside marriage. But self-deception is not altogether easy even for the world; it is practically impossible for the Christian. Hence an opposition between the Church calling for order and a world ever falling away has become a tradition for both sides. And the danger for the world is to take the matter too lightly and for the Church too seriously. I mean that Christians tend to see too much evil in relation to other evils in this straightforward vice. They tend to forget how much of it is due to weakness, bad education, difficult and unsatisfactory conditions of life. They sometimes even forget Our Lord's own readiness to forgive and understand the sinner. The world's danger, on the other hand, is to take a vice that is so easy to fall into so lightly that it can come to persuade itself that there is really no danger in it. And too late it begins to learn to its cost that demoralisation can corrupt the very morale of a people. And when this begins to happen it actually calls the Church to its aid, and asks bishops to promote public morality councils. Thus we may say that Church and world well understand each other in the matter. They have their expected rôles to play and at least they are agreed on the formula "so far but no farther."

But when it comes to other matters where there is no such clear-cut line, no such traditional rôle, the Christian is no longer faced with a measurable and clearly defined vice about which there can be no confusion. He appears in fact to be faced with good, not evil at all. Indeed he generally is faced with good, and unless he is prepared to take a long and wise view he will altogether fail to see that the world's narrowness of vision and lack of true faith must in the end cause the good to be used for disordered ends. What could be better than obedience to the law, than patriotism, than the promotion of social reform, than wider and fuller education, than the pursuit of science, than the cultivation of the arts? Faced by these the Christian congratulates the world on the pursuit of such virtues, urging even more devoted application to their pursuit, only deploring the fact that they have not been blessed by the Church. Not believing in worldly virtue, he does not see, until too late, how dangerous they can be through the fanaticism with which they are pursued. Yet it is here that both the real danger and the real opportunity are to be found. The danger, because nothing helps evil more than the good abused and disorientated; the opportunity, because nowhere does the world need more help— and in the end show itself more grateful for it—than in being furnished with a light that can show up the disorder and confusion and with a compass that can reveal the real direction in which it is making. It is not because of the degree of sexual vice, of drunkenness—which is probably less than ever before—of greed, cruelty, and lust for power —which are obvious—that so many are turning again to Christianity; it is far more because of the state of confusion in which they find themselves about apparently virtuous acts. They see good turning to evil in their hands. They see heroism and self-sacrifice and charity dedicated to destruction. They see the ancient virtues supporting despotism and tyranny. They see science and knowledge and technique inexorably building the machine that will enslave us all and destroy the very culture that builds it.

Is it surprising that when this happens there are many who turn on the Church and ask why she did not give a warning in time, why she gave a thoughtless passing blessing to so much that has in fact yielded such bitter fruit, confining her maledictions to the *effects* of disordered causes, instead of to the causes themselves? The Church which has so constantly decried sins of the flesh has tolerated nationalist passion, economic injustice, the break-up of the home, the conversion of the worker into a highly mobile instrument of production, suicidal armament races, cut-throat international and commercial competition, the denial or perversion of liberty, likewise the denial of order and authority.

It is easy to see the evil after the worst has occurred; it is not easy to see it in time. To-day we blame those churchmen who blessed the new fascism and made un-satisfactory bargains with it; but we find it quite natural that the Church should bless and approve—with narrow reservations—so many war-induced reforms and policies which may one day blossom forth as the structure of a Marxist Machine State.

(viii) DANGER IN INDEPENDENCE

But if the Church must mingle with the world, don its garments, think its thoughts, approve and foster the good in it, so must it stand apart, or else sooner or later it will be absorbed and become a Church serving the world, as

so often has happened in history, instead of the world
being guided by the Church.   The Church must be visible,
ordered, supranationally organised, authoritative, sovereign
in its own sphere.   Its worship is not simply an impulse
of the mind.   It is enshrined in all created matter, in the
bread and the wine that are to be changed into the Body
and Blood of Christ, in the stones and the mortar and the
stately forms where the sacrifice is made and the sacraments
administered, even, it may be said, in that business and
economic administration which must support the manifold
human relations between the different parts and persons.
But it is this need which presents the peculiar temptation,
whose effects were described in the beginning of this chapter.
How easy for those who have long lost all touch with the
Church and its supernatural work, who have themselves
been through a life of misery, disorder, squalor, and suffering, whose sacramental ideal has been shaped in so very
different an experience, to cry out at this otherness of the
Church, at its privileged and sheltered existence!   But how
truly sometimes can those who do not understand the
Church ask whether Christians, in their minds even more
perhaps than in their bodies, do not take undue shelter
behind this necessary structure?   It was the priest with
all his spiritual authority and his status who passed by and
left the Good Samaritan to perform the deed of mercy;
it was the Pharisee for whom Our Lord's sternest words
were reserved.   Much-abused authorities, no doubt, but
can we doubt that Our Lord meant them to teach the
inherent dangers in privilege, status, and spiritual authority,
however justified in themselves and in their proper place?
To-day, no doubt, the grosser abuses are rare.   The prelate
is not a feudal lord and the priest is rarely a man of wealth
and social state.   But I repeat that the Church is face to
face with a world of suffering, poverty, disillusion, insecurity, fear.   It is faced by a world whose best plans will

fail for want of spiritual experience. In the face of this there are more ways than one of passing-by. To be content with quoting the catechism to one who is broken and more sinned against than sinning may well be the coldest way of passing-by. How easy it is for the clerical student, perhaps himself recruited from those who have least and feel most, to climb into a different world through his education and training, to take on the characteristics of a class and caste, to come to appreciate the security and even comforts of a privileged life, perhaps one day to possess power and authority, to feel himself responsible for a complex and financially trying diocese, to taste the sweets of worldly appreciation and status, to be revered and praised for his every uttered word, to see himself as a good patriot, as an enlightened man, as a reformer—and how easy for each of these steps to draw him away from that simple human love and sympathy which prompted the Good Samaritan to perform his act of charity! And how easy for such to persuade themselves that the institution counts for more than the work for which it exists! And it is not only those who suffer in the usual meaning of the word who may be passed-by. The world is full of error and confusion, of goodness and kindliness on the eve of being turned sour. It is full of heroism and unselfishness induced by evil and disordered ends. Many a Christian himself is deeply worried about many things. But what has a priest to say to such when he has lived his life enclosed by the security of college and cloister and had his mind exclusively formed on abstract theological text-books and treatises? The worldling and the priest can only stare at one another, for they speak different languages, both having perhaps forgotten how to speak the spontaneous language of human love and sympathy.

And without going so far as those outside the Church, what of the sheep believed to be securely in the fold? It is extraordinary how content many remain with the old ways, the old well-thumbed text-books, the old modes of exercising authority, the old sermons, the old subjects, when it is patent to anyone who looks that the fold is open and the sheep escaping, with many more ready to follow.

(ix) THIS CHAPTER SUMMED UP

The world of to-day, I say, is a world attuned to heroism and sacrifice. But because it has ceased to worship God that heroism and sacrifice are offered to false gods, who rend and split and divide the worshippers, turning their good-will and high aims to hatreds, cruelties, the fanatic following of false trails, suffering of every kind. The men and women of to-day are men and women who have lived —they know what suffering means and they know the cost of achievement. However wrong they may be, this experience has been creative and valuable. However unbalanced their life, and corrupt or disintegrated in certain directions, they have in them profound potentialities of great good or great evil. Christianity cannot appeal to them by its intrinsic rightness alone, nor by its abstract order, nor its sweet reasonableness. It can only appeal if it measures itself to the heights and depths that have been lived and experienced, if it has the courage to tackle the world at its best, instead of harping on its worst. The Christian, in addition to being right, must demonstrate in living that Christian truth involves a suffering and an achievement at least as costly as that of the world of to-day. The Christian life in a richness and variety, in a depth and a height, not less real than that of the torn, ideal-seeking world, must be put forward, above all by example, as a substitute—and an infinitely better substitute—for the world failing and disintegrating despite the amazing heroism which the latter can still invoke. It is *lived and experienced* order versus lived and experienced disorder—not an abstract possible pattern versus concrete actual chaos. The abstract rightness of the Christian moral pattern is obvious enough; its realisation is the world's problem. And until Christianity is lived, even among Christians, the world will remain uninterested.

Such a position suggests a revolution—a Christian turning away from the world with the intention of erecting a new world. It suggests the kind of escape which is illustrated in revivalism, pacifism, back to the land, the founding of Christian colonies. But the Church is debarred from such escapism, because Christianity is not something other than the world; Christianity *is* the world, Christianity is the society of all men and women, all nations, all races. But it is these *reordered* so that the goodness of men can be directed towards right ideals. For Christianity there can be no short-cut. The Christian must be in the world, must be a citizen, must be a member of a country, must pursue an avocation. Somehow the Christian must solve the problem of presenting himself to the world as wholly other, with a life more intense, more real, deeper and higher and yet as one with the world, sharing *its* intensity, *its* reality, *its* depths, and *its* heights. How can that be achieved?

CHAPTER II

THE CHRISTIAN RESPONSE

(i) THE WORLD DOES NOT WANT CHRISTIANITY
WITHOUT DOGMA

OUR practical problem, then, can be stated simply enough. Allowing, first, that the contemporary world, despite the individual good-will and sufferings, patiently borne, of its men and women, is rapidly moving either towards virtual anarchy or towards a materialist totalitarianism; allowing, second, that more and more thoughtful people are desperately anxious about this trend and looking about them to see if there is any practical spiritual alternative or even leaven; and allowing, third, that Christians to-day are actually failing to meet this need—whether through their own fault, or through the fault of the world, or because no junction can be effected either for the purposes of creating a saner order through a mutual misunderstanding of the necessary conditions—what are we Christians to do about it?

At times even the orthodox and regular churchgoer who appreciates that the Church's real strength lies in her doctrine and her supernatural life is tempted to lend an ear to the unorthodox Christian reformer who calls for revolutionary changes in order to bring Christianity up to date. Let us reform the Church, root and branch, says the reformer. Let us give up the old irrational dogmas. Let us put an end to the division between the sects. Let us confine ourselves to the Sermon on the Mount and to practical Christianity in action. Let us beat the Socialist at his own game. But a fundamentally sound instinct in the contemporary man of the world makes him somewhat

2

suspicious of the contents of the flood of books that tell of "challenges to the Churches" or of "the impotence of a Christianity that might become so quickly triumphant if the author's pet prescriptions are adopted." The man of the world realises, after all, that his own interest in Christianity is the result of his increasing doubts about the latest prescriptions that decorate the shops of the booksellers or fill the columns of the highbrow papers. He feels, as I have suggested, that it is not so much evil as ignorant good-will which has been causing most of the trouble. He is therefore disappointed to find the would-be Christian reformer trying to go one better than the world, light-heartedly jettisoning the foundations of Christianity and offering yet heavier and sweeter doses of the world's own good intentions. And we can well note, as a mere fact of common experience, that these challenging books, however sincerely and intelligently written, do prove extraordinarily ineffective. They always fail to appeal to the world, which only too readily sees through the frantic efforts of their writers to make the best of what they obviously think to be a bad case; and they weaken the faith and convictions of the ordinary Christian who, if seriously disturbed by the argument, does not pause at the point painfully put forward by the author, but very soon throws up so weak-kneed a Christianity altogether.

If there is one thing that seems clear it is that when the world turns again to Christianity for help and inspiration it is moved to do so by the desire for some fundamental, unchanging, and tried principles and that it expects to hear of a hard and costly discipline. And, so far as this is the case, orthodox Catholicity possesses ultimately, I am convinced, a far greater appeal than modernism and the various brands of Christian socialism or communism.

(ii) THE WORLD IS SHY OF CHRISTIANITY BECAUSE
        CHRISTIANS ARE TOO ORDINARY—

At the same time there appear to be two main difficulties
which make the world shy of seriously interesting itself in
the Catholic answer, as it is at present being given. The
first is that the Church is too ordinary, and the second that
it is too extraordinary.

The Church tends to meet recurring world crises, even
desperate ones like the present, without any particular
excitement and scarcely an expression of surprise. That is
why it gives the impression of doing little out of the way
to meet them. While the world cannot but be impressed
by the sense of a great strength which this coolness pre-
supposes, it tends to be disconcerted, for, filled itself with
a desperate urge to find the remedy to its troubles, the *right*
path among so many promising yet deceptive paths, it
cannot understand what seems like slackness and apathy and
complacency, all the more so in that the record of Christianity does not seem so very outstanding. It is remarkable,
for example, what success can be achieved by the earnestness
and novelty of almost any brand of religious revivalism.
Right through the history of Europe we can note the
effects of Christian or near-Christian revivalism, whether
orthodox or heretical, and those effects, though generally
not destined to endure, seem out of all proportion to the
strength and means of those who preached the revived
Gospel. Before the War, for example, we had to acknowledge the appeal and widespread effects of the so-called
Oxford Group. There has been nothing striking about its
leaders, and its doctrine seems shallow and commonplace,
yet because it has at least tried to give a lead, and set a
course of action in terms of the troubles and temptations
of the contemporary world, it has caught the attention of

thousands who were content to drift unhappily in the world of contradictory ideals, greed, passion, and war. How often must it not have occurred to Catholics that if so superficial a movement could affect so many there must be something wrong somewhere with a Church which was unable, with its immense treasury of new appeals and old, even to hold on to those who have been brought up in its teaching, let alone appeal successfully to others. Imagine what might happen if behind the Oxford Group there had been the leadership, the numbers, the organisation, and the richness of appeal of the Church!

(iii) AND TOO EXTRAORDINARY

Yet the lack of popular response to the Church is certainly not solely, or even mainly, due to the Church's apparent failure to be attractive and to seem at all times desperately earnest. If the Church seems to be too ordinary, the Church also turns out to be much too extraordinary. If it is hard to pick out the Catholic, either by his behaviour or by his state of mind in regard to current political, social, and economic questions, there is no difficulty in recognising him by the things which he believes to be true and by his mode of worship. Professor Macmurray has well described one set of Catholic peculiarities. He writes: "The Church has tended to identify Christianity with a set of beliefs and theories which the development of science has made increasingly incredible. Through the whole development of science, from Copernicus to Freud, the Christian churches have been identified with the losing battle against science in defence of medieval beliefs. This has meant that millions of earnest people have been put in the position of having to choose between modern science and Christianity." Another set of Catholic peculiarities centres round sex and family morality. Here the Church's teaching about the indissolubility of marriage and the sinfulness of birth-control seems to many sincere persons seeking the light utterly unacceptable, and in its extreme interpretation wholly formalistic and unreal. And behind these two sets of difficulties there lies, I think, a yet deeper one. To put it as crudely as possible, Christianity demands a belief in God, whereas the world is still seeking salvation from a godless religion.

(iv) TWO VIEWS ABOUT GOD

I do not, of course, mean that those who look towards Christianity necessarily believe themselves to be without faith in God. On the contrary most of them would stoutly protest their faith in God, if in nothing else. But in fact most of them are a very long way from believing in God as the Catholic does. They are seeking God; the Catholic, by comparison, takes God for granted. *They* expect or hope to discover God at the end of their pilgrimage; the Catholic begins with God. It amounts to a difference of logical approach. Thus even when the individual Catholic's faith in God happens to be weak, he still retains his objective method of approach. His *Weltanschaung* (his whole way of thinking) remains in terms of God standing outside the world and himself, imposing an order or offering a pattern which man can get to know and follow. I repeat that even if the individual Catholic nurses doubts about the truth of it all, he will still base his thinking on the hypothesis of a God who reveals truth, whether through the Church or the conscience and reason. That framework makes it comparatively easy for the Catholic to accept what Professor Macmurray calls medieval belief or extremely difficult moral teachings. The emphasis throughout is on God outside who, by hypothesis, must know best. It is never on the self or the product of many selves worrying their minds about science and ethics. Not that the Catholic despises these human disciplines or studies them less ardently, but instinctively he fits their findings into God's pattern as revealed. If he cannot fit them, he supposes that there must be something wrong with himself and his fellow-men rather than with the pattern. Doubtless he admits that human reason and the discoveries of science can throw further light on the proper interpretation of the pattern, but he will not allow that the pattern can be changed. Or, if he does, he feels that his whole world has toppled over and, as likely as not, he becomes an avowed agnostic. Again this basic conviction about the otherness of God and the creature-ness of man makes it extremely easy and natural to accept traditional Christian worship in terms of sin, suffering, sacrifice, and atonement. One could scarcely expect anything else.

The modern mind, even of the naturally humble and sincere, works, I think, very differently. It is essentially subjective. It is always, as it were, manufacturing God in the workshop of the self. God is an ideal to be worked up to rather than a reality to come down from. God takes shape as the ideas of the individual mind take shape and become more coherent. It is therefore extremely difficult to accept anything as Divine (and so right and good) which does not easily fit into the workings of the mind. If an individual tends to have a logical mind, God must be very reasonable, i.e. rational; if he tends to be strongly emotional, God stands for the fulfilment of those emotions.

It would be false to suggest that many good men who see God in this way succeed only in worshipping themselves, for the human intellect, rightly used, has God for its end, and it may well be that this subjective approach reveals God in certain aspects more deeply than the average Catholic objective approach, which may tend to turn God into a formula or a code of behaviour. But it is evident that the idea of God will be limited by the capacity and sincerity of the mind which seeks Him, and that the distinction between what the self builds up to suit itself and what it actually discovers is never easily drawn. If in the best minds this approach is valuable, in the minds of most average people it can lead to serious illusions.

(v) THE CATHOLIC DIFFERS FROM OTHERS

In practice these two ways of thinking of God go far to account for the difference between Catholics and non-Catholics. The Catholic who takes God and God's order as given strikes the non-Catholic, as I have said, as too *ordinary* and too *extraordinary*. Not taking *himself*, nor the works of his fellow-men, too seriously, the Catholic is apt to seem indifferent and even cynical about the very things which trouble and distress the sincere non-Catholic. He is too ordinary. He tends to be lax about this-world political and social duties and even lax or hypocritical about moral practice. All this does not seem to matter to him terribly. He tends to departmentalise life, the things of God standing on one side, the things of this world on the other. If he becomes interested in the world's game, whether it be in business or politics, he plays it according to its own rules without scruple. Sometimes it becomes very hard to tell the difference between the Catholic and the atheist or agnostic, for both take an objective line, the first taking God too much for granted and the second denying His existence. The moral earnestness of the seeker after God who feels that the whole universe depends upon his own convictions stands in contrast to both. He is terribly serious, and he cannot take life as something of a joke, either because it seems—as it does to the agnostic—too absurdly irrational or because it is, in the opinion of the Catholic, so distorted a mirror of reality.

On the other hand the Catholic, who seems so cynical and indifferent about the troubles of the world, accepts without difficulty *extraordinary* dogmas and the most rigid of moral codes. This is God's revelation, he thinks, and it is really very silly and presumptuous on the part of man's limited intellect to deny the truth of dogmas whose very terms are beyond the reach of the human intellect. It is equally shallow to deny the truth of moral teaching which has held good and worked throughout the ages, just because it is difficult to reconcile with our feelings to-day. If the doctrine is too hard—well, man is a weak creature! Far better to stand by the truth, even though you may be too weak to live up to it, than to pretend that the truth is determined by man's weakness; far better to accept the moral teaching of the indissolubility of marriage and live with a mistress than to pretend that living with a mistress is marriage. Far better, in a word, to believe in God and serve Him badly than to serve oneself well under the delusion that one is serving God.

(vi) THE WORLD EXPECTS BELIEF AND BEHAVIOUR
TO BE CONSISTENT

Putting the contrast between the two avenues of approach in this way may help us to understand better both the lack of contact between orthodox Christianity and the world, and to find the right method of presenting to a perplexed and often sincere world the spiritual solution which still seems to many so remote and unreal.

For if the world is running along dangerous lines when it seeks God in its own beliefs, emotions, and fancies, it has at least the excuse that it can do no other. The Catholic is the first to admit that a living belief in God is a gift of God's grace, whether the grace comes with a rush, knocking one over, as in the case of Saul, or as a soft light and gentle warmth permeating the process of natural education towards an ever fuller understanding of God, man, and the universe. It is only through respect for his own deepest convictions that the non-Christian can prepare the way for understanding of the truth, and one of the factors which is very likely to affect these convictions is the behaviour and mentality of Catholics, the more so in that they make such tremendous claims. Allowing that the Catholic method of approach is the right one, we have still to bear in mind the danger of scandal. To revel in our own certainty may prove to be the most certain way of repelling the seeker after certainty. And the danger of scandal is infinitely increased when our revelling takes the form of dividing our lives into two compartments, spiritually revelling in one and worldlily revelling in the other. To behave in this way has throughout been the great Catholic danger. It is the temptation peculiar to those who are given the grace of certain faith. It was characteristic of the ages of faith and it is still characteristic of Catholic countries. Yet in both cases its effects are disastrous.

Man is one, and the non-Christian who does not see the full truth is at least right in his insistence that belief and behaviour should be integrated. His temptation is to worship whatever coherence of thought and action he can reach for himself. But we who claim to know the fuller truth, through no merit of our own, have no sort of excuse for locking it up in church and coming into vital contact with it only on Sundays. We have to learn from the non-Catholic that our actions must be integrated with our beliefs. At all events we shall not have the remotest chance of appealing to the non-Catholic, to the world, unless we try to do this.

If our faith is extraordinary, then there is nothing for it but to make our behaviour extraordinary. And in an age when the general behaviour, whether of men or countries, is at any rate extraordinary, whatever its merits, this should not seem an out-of-the-way ideal.

(vii) THE WORLD'S RHYTHM OF EXCITEMENT TO APATHY IMITATED BY CHRISTIANS

The world, I have said, is extraordinary—and it may become more extraordinary still. Not only is every tradition, every custom, every security in the melting-pot, so that no man can tell, almost from one day to the next, in what circumstances he will be living and what precise values he will be invoking, but each man is consciously or unconsciously seeking a faith. Many are already living a heroic faith. Millions to-day in every country in the world are vowed—and willingly vowed—to self-sacrifice of the highest order, the sacrifice of life itself, often with the expectation of a hideous death, and the sacrifice of all that they held dearest in the world, in the service of ideal and country. To the philosopher, historian, and theologian this faith and this sacrifice may seem largely irrational and they may well believe that it will lead to many evil consequences. Certainly it implies a contradiction, for the heroism is demanded in order to beat down the contrary idealism of opponents. If the Englishman thinks everything in Germany or Japan is hateful, we must in fairness acknowledge that the German or the Japanese thinks the same of the Anglo-American ideal. If the democrat hates the Fascist, the Fascist hates the democrat and the Bolshevik. It does not of course follow that these ideals are all equally evil, but whether good, less good, or evil we cannot but take note of the truth that they all—even those obviously evil and wrongheaded—evoke a faith, a self-sacrifice, and a heroism that is in fact sublime. The German airman burnt alive on a raid, the German soldier freezing away from his home on the plains of Russia, the German house-wife mourning her children, these are not less sublime acts of devotion, however bad the German cause, than the actions of our own countrymen.   Man can do no more.

But man is still a rational animal.   Though this or that individual can be so satisfied with a faith that he emotionally accepts and gladly dies for it, man's thinking, as it moves from generation to generation, from year to year, and from place to place, seeks for a fuller, higher, and more rational faith.   The heroics of yesterday—though the heroism in them will not be denied—become fanatical obscurantism to-morrow.   And if there is one thing which we can safely prophesy of the future it is that it will take, even in the lifetime of our own generation, a very different view of the quality of the faith which to-day is carrying millions to suffering and death.   Whichever side wins the War—and this after all is to a considerable extent the result of material accident—will damn the idealism of the opponent, but it will live to see its own idealism damned as falling very far short of whatever new order may be evolved.   And the intense reaction caused by these alterations of values, as well as by the loss of immediate stimulus to heroic action, is likely to cause a moral breakdown.   After moral exulta-tion in pursuit of irrational ends, we shall have moral slackness and selfishness in pursuit of ends that are likely to be far more rational.

Now Catholics, it seems to me, tend to follow this rhythm very closely, even though the faith that is in them should make them oppose it.   In times of war and crisis they share as wholeheartedly as their fellow-citizens both the national ideals and the actions.   In war itself they are no less brave and no less obedient than other citizens.   On the other hand, in times of peace and progress, when the best and most earnest minds are seeking a more rational way of living, Catholics are intensely critical, adopting very often a dog-in-the-manger attitude. The "ordinary" in us—that is, our somewhat cynical acceptance of the way of a godless world—is easily raised in times of war and crisis, when the world has worked itself up to conflicting but intense faiths, to the world's own extraordinary level of behaviour in pursuit of worldly ideals. Habitually, in fact, we then take the lead, and no government or ideology (except the most openly anti-Christian and persecuting) can wish for better propagandists than the Christian leaders. We then appear extraordinarily ordinary. But when the crisis is over, and statesmen, writers, and thinkers endeavour to build a saner and more progressive world, they meet with Christian resistance on the score of their lack of Christianity and their undependability in the matter of Christian dogma and Christian morals. Our "extraordinary" views about doctrine and morals stand in the way.

(viii) THE CHRISTIAN RHYTHM SHOULD BE THE OPPOSITE

When we come to analyse this double mode of behaviour, not only do we see it to be extremely ineffective, but we must admit that it is quite illogical and out of keeping with what our faith involves. For modern wars, and the great crises through which the conflicting contemporary ideologies are involved, are in fact the effect of the world's failure in quieter times to develop a more rational order, so that the Christian should logically dissociate himself from the effect, while associating himself more nearly with the efforts that are made to reach a happier solution. If, instead of condemning the world in times of relative peace and progress, just because it is "the world, the flesh, and the devil," he recognised the amount of good-will and intellectual effort that was being expended by earnest men to find constructive solutions to the problems with which they were presented, his own contribution might be studied with more attention and sympathy and with happier results. Then, above all, he should mingle with the world and impress upon it the great contribution which his Faith has to make. But when men, despairing at length of anything better, fall over one another in order to worship false and contrary faiths, and offer their lives for them, the Christian would surely create a better impression if, while recognising the degree of virtue which a false faith can evoke, and sharing the suffering and depths of experience, he stated plainly, "I told you so," and stood out conspicuously for his refusal to bow the head with the others to what is plainly false. In other words, the Christian should be extraordinarily sympathetic with a world seeking a better order and extraordinary in his refusal to fall for the consequences of any failure to shape that better world. At present he is ordinary in his indifference in times of peace and ordinary in his war-time surrender to national emotions.

(ix) CHRISTIAN APATHY TOWARDS TWO CONSTRUCTIVE URGES OF OUR DAY

Let us consider the position in more practical terms.

On the whole, during the last fifty years we can detect two great constructive "urges" in our Western civilisation. One is the "urge" towards social justice and the other the "urge" towards internationalism. The first is without any question whatsoever a movement of deep and serious moral import. The second is the reaction of common sense to the changing technique of life through science, invention, and the spread of education. The two together give—or rather gave—hope of a saner order for mankind.

On both Catholics in general frowned. It is true that from Leo XIII onwards social justice was placed in the forefront of the Church's application to society of Christian moral teaching, but Catholics themselves only very slowly accepted this lead, and to this day too many fear lest a radical change in the social order unsettle the way of the world and turn men away from a God revealed, it seems, in the established class-division of the past. In the strangest way these prejudices seem to survive the clearest proofs that the social order has had precious little to do with the will of God and a very great deal to do with the will of men who had not the slightest interest in God and God's order. They even survive the fact, staring us all in the face, that the old order is falling to pieces and that the future must either see a totally new one or deliver civilisation to the blind forces of anarchy.

Internationalism has never appealed in quite the same way as the claim to social justice, except perhaps in so far as it has been linked with the idea of an international socialist revolution. None the less there have been forces at work all the time which tend to draw men of all nations and races closer together in understanding, amity, and mutual help. But these pervasive forces have steadily given way to the much more powerful forces of international commercial competition and to an increasingly powerful sentiment of nationalism. This nationalism has in fact been openly exploited, so that disciplined peoples may be made to defend strong commercial interests. In the end, nationalism allied with commercialism grew so strong that it began to squeeze the life-blood out of the commercialism which fed it. Planned originally to protect commercial interests and groups, nationalism has turned this defence into attack, so that every economic and social interest has been swallowed up in gigantic World War, the wealth and technique of the world being devoured for the sole purpose of destroying itself. What have Catholics had to say to all this? On the whole it must be admitted that they have not protested against the trends of modern commercialism, while they have steadily supported the forces of nationalism. Inevitably therefore the weight of their influence has been *against* the forces making for a saner internationalism.

It is not pleasant to have to write this, but the truth must be faced if Christianity in the future is to respond to the chances that may be offered to it.

(X) THE REASON WHY

No doubt in recent years the difficulties before Catholics have seemed extreme, for these years have in fact marked a very rapid movement towards ideals thoroughly incompatible with Christian ends. To attempt to Christianise socialism and secularist liberalism by disentangling the good in them from the bad may have seemed a hopeless task. In fact it has often seemed to be far more important to warn the world—and many Catholics in the world—of the dangers at the heart of seemingly good and generous movements. But if this has been the case it is very largely because Christians themselves, through their too-willing acceptance of the way of the world as it had evolved from the past, had lost their own sense of Christian values. If, for example, we make a study of all the chief Papal encyclicals since the reign of Leo XIII we can extract from them admirable and secure teaching about the good and the bad in contemporary thought and movements. In them we shall find—apart altogether from their more specific spiritual direction—the proper Christian attitude towards social reform, towards education, towards science, towards economics, towards the State, towards nationalism and internationalism, towards war. Understood and made the basis of Christian action, this series of Christian charters would have given to the Christian communities the constructive lead which could have made practical Christianity an effective force during the last fifty years. It might or might not have proved decisive, but no one could doubt that a properly instructed and effectively led international body of over three hundred million people, supported by millions of other Christians, could have made a mighty difference.

Unfortunately, the first interest of the individual bishop, priest, and Catholic publicist has inevitably been, not to organise and lead forward along these lines, but rather to protect men and women already showing only too many signs of falling to the temptations of the world. To begin with, their first care has been—as it must be—to defend what is "extraordinary" about the Church—namely, its sacramental life, its doctrine, and its moral teaching. And contemporary secular movements always imply the denial of the value of all this. But, allowing for this primary duty, one may think that the need to warn the faithful against the fallacies in socialism and secularist liberalism has tended to express itself in too negative a fashion. Thus the practical condemnation has resulted in the practical acceptance of whatever may happen to be the *status quo ante*. Men, as I have said, have to live. They are obliged to accept some order. They cannot individually spin out their own ideal order as social beings and citizens. If change is condemned because of its dangers and risks, the practical consequence—unless one is very careful—is not to strive for something better, but to be content with making the best of what there is. Hence between the social teaching of Christ's Church, or even the leadership of the popes and the daily concrete practice of Christians, there has been a tremendous lag. An irresponsible dictator can greatly exaggerate his teaching in the realisation that men will follow slowly. Hence there is hope for him that practice will fall some way between the exaggerations and the old order. But this of course is impossible for the most responsible institution in the world, the Church of God. Its lead must be delicate, accurate, and precise. Hence the constant danger lest a practice, lagging so far behind necessarily responsible and cautious leadership, be actually untrue to the lead—and this in fact means being untrue to the teaching and mind of the Church.

But though all this may—and must—be said in explanation, we cannot deduce from it that a passive acceptance of the situation is inevitable. No doubt it is inevitable that the prime need to protect Christians from further contamination by disbelief and amorality will always result in a rough and ready condemnation of much good in the world with the bad, but is there any need to tolerate, if not positively to encourage, acceptance of the bad with the good in the established order? Because we suspect so much in socialism and secularist liberalism, need we tolerate so much social injustice and nationalism, as it were for old times' sake?

(xi) CHRISTIAN EXCITEMENT IN TIME OF NATIONAL CRISIS

And this brings us directly up against the opposite attitude of Christians to the times of crisis and war. Then we cease to be critical of the way of the world, and instead put ourselves forward as its most loyal citizens.

The Church, for necessary reasons, encourages Christian loyalty to the established Cæsar, readily accepts him as being the natural object of the people's loyalty to their country, and preaches the duty of serving country. And, naturally enough, the more the country is imperilled, the more ready are Christians to defend it. But in contemporary times countries are imperilled, not because of recurring dynastic quarrels or disputes over territorial possessions and commerce, but because of the ideologies and interests for which their ruling factions stand. There

enter of course into an ideology like Nazism such basic
ideals as defence of fatherland and recovery of national
prestige, but essentially Nazism, like Communism, stands
for the imposition of a way of life and a way of thinking.
It is one of the practical outcomes of the way in which men
were thinking, theorising, and behaving during the last
fifty years and more. And most of this the Church
condemned. Less obvious is the diffusion of materialistic
thinking through the Anglo-Saxon ideal, dubbed by its
opponents "plutodemocracy," but even in this case it is
not so much the historic Britain and America which are
imperilled, as a certain philosophy of social life, with its
good and its bad points.

It is true that when countries are endangered by any war
there is an instinctive return to the more fundamental
loyalties, whatever may have happened in the past. The
Germans at war feel themselves to be defending Germany
rather than Nazism, the Russians Russia rather than
Bolshevism, the British England, Scotland, Wales, the
Empire, rather than democracy. And this truth goes far
to explain the apparent contradiction of Christians rallying
in defence of ideals which in calmer moments they criticise
and condemn. On the other hand, war strengthens the
hands of the *de facto* ruling factions, and the ideologies for
which they stand are more sternly imposed. Propaganda,
moreover, which needs to appeal to the strongest feelings
of the moment as well as to what people conceive to be
the best and highest in themselves, while it bases itself on
the instinct of patriotism, endeavours to glorify the ideology
for which the country is standing. Patriotism tends to be
a negative ideal in a world where everything depends on
the *kind* of country people want, whereas Nazism or
Communism or democracy are positive ideals. They
encourage attack, aggression, a fight for total victory; they
involve hatred for the opposing ideology; they make com-

promise or negotiation impossible.   And these ideologies, even in opposition, affect one another, not by the good in the one being caught by the other, but rather by the evil.

And when we reach this kind of war, war which itself is the product of the conflict of largely false ideologies and largely selfish interests, war which demands the universal triumph of one such ideology and interest, we may well begin to ask what proportion there really remains between the Christian encouragement of defence of country and the authority of Cæsar, on the one side, and the real issues and meaning of the conflict, on the other?

My point—be it remembered—is not to urge at this stage that the Church or that Christians ought to take up a different attitude; I am here concerned rather to find out why the world pays so little attention to the Church, and seeking to analyse the reasons why Christians behave *ordinarily*, instead of *extraordinarily*. And surely the instinct of thinking men, more especially those many persons who find themselves involved in this strange medley of contradictory ideals for which civilisation is so gallantly sacrificing itself, is against a Church which, on the one side, offers a magnificent, coherent, and extraordinary ideal, but which, on the other, accepts with so little apparent difficulty wholehearted action in defence of these very contradictions!

(xii) THIS CHAPTER SUMMED UP

Let me briefly sum up again.

Why is it that Church and world fail to connect?   I suggest, first, that it is not because the Church refused to throw up her doctrine and supernatural life, as extreme reformers are apt to demand.   Still, the world is repelled by the fact that Christianity appears at once too ordinary and too extraordinary—too indifferent about this-world concerns and too remote in its startling doctrinal claims and its rigid moral code. This separation between "week-day" indifference and "Sunday" fervour tends to be a characteristic of men who begin by believing in God and God's revelation and then seek to fit life into God's pattern. For them no revelation is too difficult to believe, but for them also the troubles, anxieties, problems that constitute the staple daily anxiety of the earnest man of the world seem of little importance. Hence the latter takes scandal at the Christian. He demands a closer correlation between faith and practice—and in so far he is right.

Therefore, since Christians cannot bring the extraordinary in them down to the level of the ordinary, they must raise the ordinary up to the level of the extraordinary.

But this is not what Christians have done. On the contrary they have tended to remain indifferent to the world's attempts to seek social justice and international collaboration, on the grounds that the world was not supernaturally guided and often seemingly hostile to religion (they invoked the extraordinary in themselves as an excuse for being ordinary). But when the world reaps the consequences of its failure (partly due to the Church's lack of interest and sympathy) to create a better order, and sinks into ideological revolution and war, Christians find no difficulty in playing their fullest parts as citizens in the ideological struggles between erroneous and inadequate faiths (like others, they become extraordinary ordinary).

In all this, I repeat, I have not sought to judge, nor to establish whether or not this behaviour is justified or inevitable. I have merely tried to account for the reasons why in fact the Church makes an insufficient impression on the world of to-day.

CHAPTER III

THE WAY OF "WISDOM"

(i) THAT COURAGE AND SELF-SACRIFICE FOR RELIGION
ARE NOT ENOUGH FOR THE WORLD

I HAVE suggested that if we want the world to interest
itself in the "extraordinary" in the Church, we must do so
by being "extraordinary," not only about extraordinary
things, but about ordinary ones. We cannot offer a
supernatural ideal—and this after all *is* the Christian ideal—
and expose it solely on Sundays or when everything is
quiet. The priest who carries the Blessed Sacrament
under a worn and tattered coat into the trenches, through
the slums, to plague-infected hospitals symbolises the
mission of Christianity. Yet in a way it is easier to live
a priestly life of apostolic heroism according to the never-
failing tradition of the Church than to live, day in and day
out, an ordinary Christian life which forms as it were a
living monstrance of the supernatural; and hardest ideal
of all, perhaps, is the ideal of the Church of Christian
peoples, set in the world as *the* monstrance of God's
presence in our midst, of His Will, of His plan, of His help.

The priest who carries the Blessed Sacrament through
physical dangers to the least of his brethren is doing a
simple and straightforward act, however courageous it
may be—but courage, as we have seen, is not a rare virtue—
especially to-day. Such a priest may or may not at ordinary
times be a man of great spiritual devotion, and he may or
may not be a man of wisdom. Let us allow that he is a
man of great spiritual devotion, an ascetic, and a man of
prayer. Far be it from me to depreciate a devotion and
asceticism for which I myself have neither the strength of

will nor the courage—still further be it from me to seem
to criticise what is after all the imitation of Christ and of
Christ's saints, the more so in that it is plain that the world
—though it may sometimes outwardly sneer—is looking
for personal devotion and idealism in the highest things
which man can follow, equal to the devotion and idealism
so often wasted upon temporal and often dangerous ends.
The example of one man of heroic life and virtue can and
does have immeasurable influence, while the many men and
women dedicated to God in contemplative communities of
rigorous observance not only do immense good by their
prayers and self-sacrifice, but keep alive the ideal of a holy
and useful social life, of a spiritual cell, in marked contrast
with the disorder, materialism, and self-indulgence of the
world.   The rest of us indeed must be sustained to some
kind of petty effort towards God's service by the inspiration
of the single-minded servants of God in religious and lay
life.

None the less I suggest—not as a higher ideal but perhaps as a harder one, and certainly as a complementary
one of no less importance—that to-day, when the contrast
is so often between a courageous, but misguided, world
and Christians, faithful in the "extraordinary" side of their
vocation rather than inspiring in its "ordinary" side, the
demand is also insistent for something that I shall call
wisdom rather than mere devotion or asceticism.   This is
certainly rarer.

(ii) HARDER TO LIVE CHRISTIANITY THAN TO
DIE FOR IT

Courageous priests to carry the Blessed Sacrament
wherever it is asked for, or to administer the Last Sacraments
without a thought for their own lives, are to be found in
plenty.   Indeed it is a glory of the Church that a man may

search for many months and not find a priest who would refuse to face any risk to minister the Church's sacraments to those in need. But, I repeat, what sailor, what soldier, what airman will refuse to-day to run similar risks in the service of his country when duty calls? And even among the ranks of the untrained Civil Defence Workers heroism of this order has become common. The Church's shame in this sphere of simple courage is too often to be found among the laity, whose cowardice is often such that they actually prefer not to be known publicly as Catholics lest their companions think the less of them or dub them "pious." How many are willing to fight Christianity's battle even in plain issues like those of education? Even so, one likes to think that if it ever came to the test of persecution, and even martyrdom, a high percentage of these would, with God's grace, be found willing to endure and suffer. For, as has been often said, it is easier to suffer and die for a cause than to live for it. It is easier because the issue is simpler and clearer. It is a case of all or nothing, rather than a case of weighing up in delicate balances.

And so long as we are concerned with devotion and asceticism, we are still dealing with comparatively plain and simple issues. The man or woman who follows a religious vocation is set a straightforward task, however hard it may be for human nature to live up to it. His job is to steer clear of the world, except for precise times and occasions when he must cross the bridges into the world in order to give the world the spiritual help for which he is trained. And even though these times and occasions be many—as in the case of the secular priest—nine-tenths of his actions follow a clear and practical programme. His real life, his own life, is concentrated upon the specifically spiritual. Though the layman can never be so separated from temporal concerns, such as earning a living, bringing up a family, taking part in social and national life, it still remains possible for some to concentrate so completely on the life of devotion that these temporal cares become almost matters of pure habit. At any rate the spirit is only very secondarily concerned with them, and, so long as gross sin is avoided, they are taken for granted. This does not mean that they will not be well done—on the contrary, they are likely to be very well done, because the set rules are followed conscientiously and simple-mindedly. There is little perplexity and doubting on the part of a mind primarily devoted to other-worldly interests. Thus we often find that the saintly man makes an excellent soldier or sailor or diplomat or civil servant—and in these professions is indistinguishable from others.

But all this, I suggest, taken by itself—whether it be the courage of the man who lives up to his religious duty or the asceticism and devotion of the man who lives for "the things of God" alone—still falls short of something which the world to-day especially needs and is looking for. All this still fails to build up the perfect monstrance that can exhibit to the fullest advantage the Church's spiritual treasure. For the monstrance—if I may so put it— remains turned away from the world and turned towards Heaven. I am not forgetting that it is grace—God's own action upon the soul, and upon the world through the souls of men—which alone helps, and that it is through prayer, spiritual discipline, and the practice of the fullest submission to God's will that this grace is obtained. None the less the monstrance of which I have spoken carries God Himself, God in the Sacramental Presence, God in His Mystical Body, God through the Sacrifice of the Mass and the Sacraments. Surely this means that it should be turned *towards* the world, carried through the world, taken into every hole and corner of the world, and taken daily, through every avocation and by every Christian. It is God who acts throughout, but He has left it to the

Church and the faithful to prepare the way for His passage. Is this special work fulfilled so long as little is done to bridge the gap between Church and world? Does one not sometimes get the impression that the best of Christians are more concerned to entrench themselves in their elevated Promised Land, letting down numberless ropes to the lower world, calling down instructions about how best to climb the ropes of salvation, praying that those who attempt the climb may not fall, rather than themselves take the risk of going down among their brethren that God's way may be prepared in the outer darkness?

That is why I suggest that the way of wisdom must be added to the way of courage and devotion. I need hardly say that many Christians—and all the real saints—have added this way of wisdom. But I am now dealing with the hundreds of thousands of Christians who manifest courage and who do sincerely strive to go some way along the path of spiritual perfection, but to whom this point of view may be somewhat novel. I said above that the hardest ideal of all is the ideal of the Church as a whole acting as a monstrance of God's presence in our midst. By that I meant, of course, the phenomenal Church, the Church *as it appears* to men of the world. This is the Church of the daily life, activities, sayings of its clerical leaders, of its more prominent lay-folk, of its clergy, of its millions of unpresuming faithful, of its institutions, its schools, its good works. Among all these there is courage and personal holiness and rigid principle (extraordinary virtues on extraordinary occasions and in exceptional situations), all of which the world acknowledges freely, but is there a sufficiency of wisdom, the grace to be extraordinary, and to take what often seems to others an extraordinary point of view, in ordinary life?

(iii) THE WAY OF WISDOM DEMANDS A CONSTANT EFFORT TO JUDGE AS A CHRISTIAN

By wisdom I mean the ability to judge of the worth of *all* human activities in accordance with God's pattern and the habitual practice of acting in terms of this judgment.

But this way, it may sound like a tremendous and impossible ideal, if not an ideal full of presumption. But, when all is said and done, it *is* the ideal of the ordinarily sincere and conscientious man, and it is he whom the Church must impress. When any man is at his best, and in so far as he is at his best, he makes his decisions and carries out his duties in accordance with *his* best judgment. He asks what he ought to do; he weighs up the likely consequences of each course of action; he sets these expectations against his highest standards; he takes his decision and follows his course, at all times bearing in mind these values. In most cases his chief trouble arises from the lack of fixed standards rooted in God's revelation through the Church and through his own rightly used God-given reason. And, maybe, he does not possess the courage or training to live up to what he knows to be best. In the case of Catholics these standards and this essential knowledge are given; what is too often lacking is the interest and training in *applying* those standards and knowledge to every problem and circumstance of life. The man of the world *has* to think for himself, if he wishes to act intelligently at all, for there is no one to think for him; *the Christian is in danger of never thinking for himself because he expects all his thinking to be done for him.*

But the truth is that no one—not even God—can do a man's thinking for him, for to refuse to think would be to refuse to be a man. In evading an issue, man still makes *his* personal choice, though that choice is then reduced to a kind of negative quantity, and man uses his humanity in order to be less of a man and more a victim of his environment. God has revealed what we need to know of the truth. God's Church, through the teaching of the Vicar of Christ and the successors of the Apostles, through doctrine and tradition and reason, sufficiently interprets that truth so that we are always directed and guided in vital matters. All men in authority and responsibility, whether in Church or State or society, have the duty of leading within the measure of their authority and preparing the way for others. But in the end it is the individual person himself who *lives*, and who in living should apply to this and that and that unique and unrepeatable occasion, the knowledge and training which he has acquired. He and he alone has to make the choice. And even though he takes the trouble to guide himself again and again and again with the help of confessor or friend or teacher—or even if he tries to avoid deciding for himself—the choice, the act itself, with its own unique character, is always his own.

All this is obvious enough, though far too often forgotten in practice, but it is not so obvious that if we think not of one individual person only so acting, but of Christians in general so acting, we obtain in the aggregate a certain atmosphere, a certain habit, a certain way of looking at things which can greatly vary in quality at different times. It may be better or worse according to the worth of the judgments that are all the time being made. Even though the Church is Divinely protected, and even though the teaching remains the same, the tone or character of the Church as represented by the body of Christians changes from age to age and even place to place. Always these unique personal judgments or decisions are being taken—

taken by popes, taken by bishops, taken by priests, taken by lay-folk, taken by saints, taken by sinners. But if there is—as I suggest there is—a constant habit on the part of Catholics, and often other Christians, to make these decisions, as it were, passively or negatively by reference solely to a higher authority, by the wooden application of a spiritual or moral rule of thumb, there will be a progressive tendency for the whole body of Christians to fall back more and more on the strongest and most obvious and simplest influences. The centre of gravity, as it were, of Christian action will move, slowly but steadily, in one—and that the safest and most conservative—direction. The Church will tend, or seem to tend, to use the modern jargon, to be "escapist," to evade rather than to face the full responsibilities of the times.

This, it seems to me, is what does take place. The formal knowledge of God, the abstract pattern of order with its simple code of conduct, is so strong in the Church that the habitual action, the mode, the atmosphere of Christian life is more and more weighted in one direction, that of a closed supernatural and moral system. And, as a consequence, the life of the Church tends to lose its dynamism and spontaneity and contact with ordinary living and ordinary ideas. Thus within the selfsame Divinely founded and infallible Church there can be a very wide gap between a state in which Christians habitually judge on wrong motives, or refuse to judge for themselves at all if they can help it, and a state in which they consciously and responsibly seek to judge in terms of a Christian ideal applied to the changing world around them.

Let it not be supposed that this analysis involves the slightest criticism of the doctrine or authority of the Church, for the question of error there does not arise at all. It is rather a question of the *best* use of the knowledge and grace which God bestows on the Church and her members.

It is a question of more perfect co-operation, the kind of co-operation needed to-day. Even if action is correct or sufficient, the ideal is not to act just *because* someone else tells one to, but to act for oneself *because one sees for oneself*, in the light of God's will and the teaching of the Church or one's lawful superior, that the action *is* right. Each action should be a spontaneous living expression of personal choice and responsibility, properly determined by all the circumstances. To try to evade personal responsibility by throwing the responsibility upon another is far more of an act of rebellion than freely to express in oneself and for oneself the will of God as properly interpreted through authorities representing God, for the attempt to evade responsibility involves taking to some extent a blind plunge. As I have said, each human act is a unique choice. By throwing the responsibility upon someone else you do not really evade making a choice, you choose to act blindly, and your particular habit, passion, idiosyncrasy inevitably counts for much in the act. By freely and personally doing the will of God as expressed through the Church, civil authority, reason, and as applied to this particular act, you are acting in perfect and intelligent submission to what is much greater than yourself.

When then I say that "wisdom" means the ability and habit of judging of the worth of human activities in accordance with God's pattern, I mean that every human act should be a free, personal, intelligent choice in the light of all the circumstances, in which of course the most important will be the teaching of God's Church and the proper authority of God's delegates. But this is a very different thing from being content to close one's eyes and "follow my leader," however great and good the leader.

(iv) THE CHURCH'S COMMISSION IS LIMITED, BUT NOT THE INDIVIDUAL CHRISTIAN'S

I have suggested that if in a large society all the members are content to evade their own personal responsibility, by blindly following someone else, the net result is a progressive strengthening of certain deeply entrenched and essentially conservative (and to some extent out-of-date) characteristics. Now the Church was instituted by Christ for a very special and highly important purpose. The Church is the guardian of the Revelation entrusted to it. The Church has Divine Authority to teach truth in Faith and Morals. Through the Sacraments instituted by Christ, and put into operation by the Church, mankind is provided with the normal channel for the obtaining of God's grace and therefore of salvation. If we believe in God at all, and in a supernatural order, nothing could be of greater importance than all this. Even so, it is not everything. In God's pattern the Church has a paramount place, but the pattern and the Church are not one. Man's life on earth is also concerned with temporal matters. These temporal matters must fit into a supernatural pattern, but in order to do so they themselves must first fit into the temporal pattern that is natural to them. Otherwise a man who believes himself to be in a state of grace might argue that he will do without food altogether, for then he will die and go at once to heaven. It would however be wrong to do this, because it would imply that temporal things can be squeezed into the spiritual pattern while themselves remaining disordered in their own nature. It would involve two kinds of truth, a lower or temporal truth which is of no real importance, and a higher or supernatural truth which alone counts. But truth is one, and the supernatural order is only the Divine blessing and perfecting of the temporal order. Hence God's pattern involves, first of all, the ordering of temporal matters according to their natural ends—and this is not the work of the Church as such. Since man is ignorant and fallible, and since the temporal order should always be moving towards its fulfilment in the supernatural order, the Church, acting in God's name, is ever deeply concerned with this ordering of temporal matters, reminding men of their true end, setting up red danger signs, guiding, helping. But the work itself falls on man and on the temporal societies which men form. The Church has no commission to tell statesmen how they shall conduct their business of State—though it must tell them when their conduct is so disordered that it cannot possibly fit into God's pattern. The Church has no commission to tell the artist how he should paint his picture— though it must tell him when the picture is either harming him (by, for example, absorbing all his mind to the exclusion of equally important concerns) or harming others.

(v) GOD PROVIDES A "SHORT-CUT" TO SALVATION, BUT IT DOES NOT WORK FOR SOCIETY AS A WHOLE

If we look then at human affairs as an infinitely complex and ever-changing kaleidoscope, which must nevertheless be ordered according to an equally complex pattern of sub-patterns; and if we remember that each action in the moving design must be performed by individual persons, guided, it is true, by authority, but even so largely condemned to something more like trial and error because of the complexity of the present and the darkness of the future, we get an idea of the task that faces us and our fellow-men at any moment in history. Happily God has not left us wholly at the mercy of such circumstances, for each human life is, as it were, to some extent detachable from its environment, and it is given the opportunity of reaching its proper end by a sort of "short-circuiting" the pattern as a whole. A man can save his soul without saving the whole world. Now the Church's first concern is to afford God's special help to individual men and women to some extent apart from the complexity of the whole design. By keeping certain simple rules, by behaving in a manner that is within the limits of their powers, God, either directly or through the Church, can save them as individual souls. But this "short-circuiting" process of personal salvation is not a kind of trick; it remains inter-related with the long and never-ceasing struggle of mankind as a whole to work out the complete pattern. The order that is necessary for personal salvation is the same order as God wills for the world as a whole. And man, whether he likes it or not, remains tied to the world, his actions, character, mind being continuously, profoundly, influenced by the world and his fellow-men.

Should the world be in a state of peculiar disorder, he also will be largely disordered, and it will be harder for the individual to attain to that minimum order necessary for salvation. His life will be all the more torn and twisted, spiritually, socially, physically. Even more important, in such a deeply disordered world it will be much harder for the majority of men to see the "short-cut" to salvation through the Church or through their own fidelity to conscience. Lastly that state of disorder is evil in itself, since it is in living conflict with God's will, and therefore it becomes even more the duty of men to seek to remedy it. We cannot save our souls without doing something about it—without charity towards our fellow-men.

On the other hand, there will be an inevitable temptation for those who have special knowledge of the "short-cuts," and special authority to teach them, to propose an abandon-ment of the apparently hopeless task of reordering the world and to encourage a concentration on the "short-cut."

There will be a temptation to think only of the comparatively simple and plain work of individual salvation in spite of the world. And the tendency will be for individuals to blind themselves to the full complexity of the situation, remaining content instead to "follow their leaders" along a safer path to be negotiated under expert guidance.[1]

In other words, men who know the essential truth will, under these circumstances, tend to avoid making choices in the light of all the circumstances and they will become accustomed to allow their betters to make safe choices for them. They will seek to escape having to grope their way in semi-darkness and surrounded by every obstacle and danger; instead they will look up to the steadier and stronger light, which, none the less, only reaches to certain favoured spots.

(vi) THE "SHORT-CUT" DOES NOT IMPRESS A WORLD WHICH HAS LOST FAITH IN DOGMA

It is not for a simple Catholic writer to sit in judgment and attempt to say whether or not the Church at any particular time is right to concentrate on the short-cut and abandon the world so much to its own disordered devices, but the task I have set myself is to inquire why in fact the Church does fail so largely to make its appeal to-day, even to good men in the world who are desperately seeking for the light. And for this purpose it is permissible to try to analyse the situation, without passing judgment. And here—so it seems to me—we find a real clue.

The Christian, for sufficient or insufficient reasons (that is not my concern), does not habitually judge and act in

[1] It may be contended that when Christendom broke up, after the Reformation, Christians tended to despair of the world and to concentrate on a purely personal salvation. It is only through the evidence of an increasing worldly disorder that Christianity is beginning to realise again that personal salvation is closely bound up with the salvation of society as a whole.

the light of all the circumstances. Instead he jumps to a short-cut, known only to himself. He is capable of immense courage in standing up for his views and in acting in their light; he often manifests heroism, determination, and self-mastery in following *his* path to salvation; but he refuses to apply what he knows to all the circumstances, and thus his life becomes, to the rest of the world, not an example of what ought to be done (or at least tried), but an example of how a difficulty can be overcome, *if you happen to share the secret.*

But the trouble to-day is that the world has lost the secret and cannot easily find the way to recover it. It has lost it precisely because the Christian has lost interest in saving it.

The world to-day clearly no longer believes, nor is disposed to believe, in the "extraordinary" in the Church. For the most part it does not really believe in God; while the dogmas and sacraments of the Church are regarded as medieval superstitions totally incompatibile with modern scientific knowledge. The world realises its own great disorder; it is presented with a picture of self-destruction owing to the clash of obviously false ideals; it is perplexed to find so much goodness and devotion turned into the instrument of evil—but it cannot accept (because it cannot believe) the Church's solution. Not only that, but it is often scandalised to notice a lacuna between the professions and the apparent practice of Christians who seek their own way of salvation, while so often participating in the evil way of the world, as though the latter did not greatly matter.

Surely at a time like this a great and serious effort should be made, on the part of all Christians, so to think and act in temporal and worldly affairs as to bring, first, the wisdom and moral sense of the Church and, second, its secret treasury, its true spring of life, into the market-place.

Surely the Church, as represented by its faithful of all degrees, should become a living monstrance of God's presence, light, and grace turned all the time to the world and carried through it.   And this perpetual act of daily "de-monstration" of God's Truth can only be accomplished in the lives and thoughts and daily attitudes of the members of the Church of all degrees.   This involves the resolution of all not to retreat from the world, not to be content to seek personal salvation along a secure, simple, and hidden path, not to be content with living by rote or habit according to a mere established custom; *it involves, on the contrary, the resolution to apply fearlessly and by ever-repeated and ever-changing personal judgments the inspiration, teaching, and values of Christianity to every circumstance in which the Christian may find himself.*   This alone can re-arouse the world's curiosity about the Church's secret.

(vii) THE RESPONSIBILITY IS ON INDIVIDUAL CHRISTIANS, NOT THE CHURCH

This is a task, let us remember, which the Church *as such* cannot accomplish.   The Church's spiritual and supernatural mission is limited to Our Lord's definite commission.   The Church teaches, guides, and offers the normal way of salvation, but the Church does not enter —except by way of guidance and warning—into temporal, political, economic, social, cultural, artistic affairs.   It is the Christian person, the member of the Church, and the citizen of the world, who enters into these in virtue of the oneness of his personality, which is temporal as well as spiritual.

The individual choices of action in circumstances affecting the temporal and spiritual together—and what circumstances do not?—are made, not by the Church, but by human persons, many of whom profess Christianity.   These persons alone can know the whole particular circumstances, and these persons must either turn a blind eye, acting passively, by imitation or habit, or they must seek to form their own judgment, which in each case must of necessity go some way beyond what can be laid down in prescriptions and text-books. And in such action it may well be that the best inspiration will not come from the static rule alone, but rather from the sense of being the living member of a Body, a Body alive, moving, working, looking to the future in an ever-changing process, the Mystical Body of Christ. For it is the vocation of all of us to be other Christs. Christ Himself, though God, was limited as Man by time and space. He moved in the world of Galilee and He made His judgments and took His actions in terms of His own environment and circumstances. Though their meaning and lessons were universal, the choices themselves were particular. And Christ, knowing this, rather than leave His followers to their own unguided choices, founded the Church, which through the ages has preserved and amplified and brought His universal teaching up to date. But even the enduring Church cannot relieve the individual Christian of his duty to try to be "another Christ" among his fellow-men in those special, unique, and unforeseeable circumstances through which every new life is lived. With the inspiration of Christ Himself as model, with due submission to the authority of the Church which Christ founded, as a member of Christ's Mystical Body, the Christian still has to use his own best judgment as to the Christ-like behaviour in thought and action which repeatedly novel situations demand.

I am not forgetting the fallibility and ignorance of us all, and I am not trying to suggest that with a wave of a wand we can all become wise saints, truly "other Christs." If that were practicable there would indeed be no problems before either Church or State. My point is the much more modest one that this ideal of personal action after God's pattern in the light of all the circumstances should be set before us if we want the world to attend to us. It is not enough to-day, I suggest, that we should stick to the "extraordinary" in our faith; it is not enough even that we should try to lead personal lives of devotion and asceticism in supernatural matters; we must also seek Christian wisdom. We must, as citizens, family men, business men, craftsmen—in a word, as men of the world—judge and behave as becomes persons possessing a whole philosophy of life that can, first, reorder what is disordered in temporal and worldly affairs, and, second, fit that natural order into the greater and wider supernatural order. If we try to evade this duty, if we leave it to others, if we are content passively to follow a leader who in his turn follows another leader, this work of constant and never-ceasing adjustment of the temporal and the spiritual will never take place, and the gap between Church and world will grow wider and wider. The Church will tend to lead its own set supernatural life—which of course is its first duty, and the one upon which it must concentrate when persecution deprives it of liberty—while Christians themselves will lead their daily lives in accordance with secularist philosophies, parts of which may just be tolerable but which as a whole are hopelessly non-Christian; and the world (not understanding that supernatural life which seems to the unbeliever more like magic than religion) will lose all contact with God's revelation, which is hidden in the sacristy and not to be discerned in the daily lives of Christians who apparently are not so very different in their values from other men.

(viii) AN EXAMPLE TAKEN FROM CHRISTIAN PACIFISTS

Let me take an example that is exceedingly appropriate to the times, the example of the Christian attitude towards war.

This, as we know, is a very awkward and difficult topic, but that is no reason for evading it.   A number of Catholics call themselves Christian pacifists.   I may say, lest it be supposed that I am arguing my own case, that I personally do not agree with them, though I do think that they are far nearer the Christian truth than those who have no scruple whatever in accepting the whole "bag of tricks" of nationalist and ideological values which lead to war and feed it, once it has begun: the deification of country as man's supreme loyalty; international economic competition for the strength, glory, and empire of the nat.on; exploitation of colonial peoples and possessions; utilisation of smaller peoples as instruments of the policy of larger ones; propagation of hatred against a potential or actual rival; the use of any methods of warfare to obtain victory with the sole sanction of the danger of the enemy using the same methods against oneself; conviction that peace is unobtainable until an enemy is completely crushed, and so on.   My point, however, is that the Christian pacifists, whether rightly or wrongly, have tried to face the situation on its merits and have made a personal judgment of a temporal situation in the light of Christian values, as they see them.   They have not shut their eyes; they have not evaded their responsibility as Christians and citizens.   Nor on the other hand can it be said that they have argued and thought irresponsibly.   They appeal to Christian theology, philosophy, and history.   To frown on them as dangerous Christians because they try to live and apply Christianity— and yet in due submission to authority—is to frown on precisely the kind of Christian attitude that will earn the respect and interest of the world.

But—it will be objected—they do not act with the authority of the bishops.   Of course they do not, because the bishops could not accept their arguments unless they themselves were perfectly satisfied that the Christian pacifist case were so clear and compelling that it must be taught as the duty for *all* Christians. To suggest this is to suggest that the Christian pacifist case is far clearer than it is—indeed that it is the only possible Christian case. Obviously it is nothing of the kind. It may be that in another generation or two, when a fuller realisation of the course and meaning of contemporary secularist philosophy inter-penetrates the substance of the Church, Christian pacifism will become more generally accepted. But if this develop-ment should take place—which is very far from certain—it will be because Christian persons have of their own accord made their prior personal judgments in the matter. Such developments are processes of growth in the life of an organism. They take place slowly and through subtle changes in its cells. It may be that a modified pacifism will grow through more and more Christians thinking for themselves and being forced to this conclusion; it may be that God will send a saint who will live this Christian pacifism and stir the rest of the faithful. I personally should suggest that, if this development were ever to come, it would be through more and more Christians becoming *total* Christians, not merely in regard to the particular question of war, but also in regard to related issues of economics, industry, social matters—for there seems to me to be something suspicious about Catholics who take an intransigent attitude to war, but are apparently perfectly content to lead their business lives and maintain their investments in a social order that, judged by the same standards, is equally un-Christian.

However all this may be, the Christian pacifist has acted as a Christian. He has tried to apply *for himself* his Christianity to temporal affairs. He has been prepared to suffer for his views. And this sincerity and courage, whether objectively justified or not, has surely left its impression on the body of the Church. But, from the point of view of my argument, his behaviour has an even more important aspect; the Christian pacifist has done something which strikes the world. He has been "extra-ordinary" in a matter of ordinary life. He has carried Christ into the market-place. No doubt the immediate reaction in time of war may be partly hostile, but one has little patience with those who are only interested in a Christianity which obtains the plaudits of a war-frenzied crowd. Nothing is easier in time of war than to become a hero of the hour. Give yourself over to the Ministry of Information, add a religious halo to its arguments, and the trick is done. But those who are impressed by this are not the people who to-morrow will matter to Christianity. These very same people, having been converted by circum-stances from a war hysteria to some liberal or progressive or socialist hysteria, will be the first to denounce the bellicose Christians for having betrayed Christian ideals in war-time. The sincere people who are perturbed and puzzled, the sincere people who are looking for an answer, and looking sometimes in the direction of Christianity, may well be more impressed by a handful of Christian pacifists—even though they do not agree with them—than by the body of nationalist-ridden Christians.

(ix) CHRISTIANS AND THE JUSTICE OF WAR

And let us look at the matter from a broader angle. If we cannot accept the Christian pacifist position, we shall at least be impressed by the argument that a Catholic may not participate in an unjust war of aggression. Yet millions of Catholics in Germany have apparently little scruple of conscience in serving a dictatorship which persecutes at home and commits criminal acts of aggression in international affairs. We know the excuses made. The matter does not appear in the same light to the Germans, who have found the only way of breaking a blockade and seeking redress for the injustice of Versailles. And are not German Catholics serving their country in Christian patriotism?

This is not the place to argue the rights and wrongs of the question, but one has the right to ask whether there is much evidence in Germany or Italy or Spain [1] of a Christian conscience in regard to the War. The issue may be sufficiently doubtful to allow of the bishops remaining passive, save only where the direct supernatural interests of the Church are concerned. But is this to be counted as permission to all Catholics to cease to think for themselves? Are we to suppose that some thirty or forty million Catholics are freed from the duty to judge for themselves in a grave and complex question just because the issue is not clear enough for an authoritative decision? In my contention, the fact that the matter is apparently so regarded constitutes a terrible Christian weakness. It goes far to account for the world's lack of interest in a Church which, whatever its sources of spiritual strength, does not act upon them in the precise issues which, above all, vex the world.

I have taken certain war issues as examples because they are striking at the present time. But I might have been less controversial and have pointed out how Christian doctrine and morals are neglected or unimaginatively applied by the "good" Christians. Dorothy Sayers has shown in a magnificent pamphlet, *The Other Six Deadly Sins*, how the Christian in concentrating on the sin of Lust has almost lost interest in the very meaning and relevance of Wrath, Gluttony, Covetousness, Envy, Sloth, and Pride. If the Christian awoke again to the meaning of these, the respectable names by which they go to-day

---

[1] I have chosen these countries because the argument, as applied to them, has an obvious force. But—whatever conclusion we may reach—the problem also occurs in our own case.

and their wide applicability to our most habitual actions and states of mind, the world would be faced with a very different Christian phenomenon.

So long as matters do not change, so long as the monstrance is turned away from the world and carried well above it, rather than through it, can we be surprised at the fact that a world which has lost its supernatural faith is also unable to find the way back to it?

(x) THIS CHAPTER SUMMED UP

Summing up a simple and straightforward chapter, it is sufficient to recall that the courage, devotion—asceticism— of the Christian in the extraordinary things of his Faith are not enough to impress and interest the world.   Courage is a fairly common virtue, especially to-day, and the devotion and asceticism are turned away from the world.

The Church and Christians should be a monstrance carrying Christ and Christ's order into the world's market-place.   This is a task difficult to accomplish so long as Christians tend to see Christian life as a mere obeying of authority, with the danger that they will form the habit of relying solely on authority and evading that personal judgment of daily life in which the teaching and spirit of the Church (Christ's ideal) is applied here and now to the particular and unique set of circumstances in which a man finds himself.   To do this is not to make less of authority, but more of authority, for it is the only practical way of applying authority to every circumstance of life.   The Church as such cannot do it for us, because the Church is not commissioned to do so, nor could she be made aware of every changing circumstance.   But Christians, who are citizens, artists, business and professional men, as well as religious men, can and should.   By seeking to do so, not only will they interest and impress the world with the meaning of Christianity, and its practical implications, but they will be constantly strengthening, filling out, enriching the Church of God. An example of practically applied Christianity is afforded to-day by Christian pacifists, whether they are justified or not; an example of a Christianity that is not practically applied is afforded by those who accept uncritically national propaganda and conduct in regard to war.

CHAPTER IV

THE CHURCH IN ACTION AND WHAT SHE IS FACING

(i) THE CHURCH PRESENTS A FINE PICTURE

A SURVEY of the Christian world to-day surely affords striking evidence of the Christian failure to demonstrate the impact of Christianity upon the problems that most urgently vex the best of men.

Let us not exaggerate or allow ourselves to fall into the trap which ensnares so many emotional and unorthodox Christian reformers. The Church is there. The Church is at work. The Church offers to those who seek ample evidence of its holiness and apostolicity. In Rome the Pope speaks. He speaks again and again and upon all subjects. Someone indeed should set himself the task of studying each major Papal pronouncement since the publication of Pius IX's *Quanta Cura* in 1864 to the latest Christmas Allocution of Pius XII, comparing them, relating them together, translating them into more familiar and homely language, and publishing the result as the "Voice of the Popes." [1] We should all be taken by surprise in

[1] While these pages were in the press, *The Popes' New Order*, by Father Philip Hughes, was published. It goes far to meet the need.

realising the amplitude, the fullness, the completeness, often the revolutionary quality, of the lead of the modern Papacy. Unfortunately it has too often been left at that, for this leadership has not permeated through the body of the Church, except where it concerns directly dogmatic, moral, and devotional matters.

Nor should the latter be underrated.   The Church to-day across the face of the globe presents a picture of men and women at prayer and work, of men and women leading, in the face of increasing worldly temptation, lives of asceticism, sacrifice, and moral rectitude often amounting to the heroic degree, of men and women supported and comforted in every trial by a burning faith in God, of men and women ready to face any and every danger in furtherance of their apostolic mission.   All this may apply only to a minority of Christians, but it is a large minority, and absolutely it includes a very great number of souls.   As for the others, it is no small matter that they also, when it comes to a real test, turn more fully to the ministrations and help of the Church of God.   To be fair, however, we must not overlook the unhappy picture of drift, a drift away that cannot be accurately measured, but about which all competent investigators are deeply anxious.

(ii) BUT STILL IT IS OBVIOUSLY NOT ENOUGH—
REASONS WHY

The fact remains that this fine picture—finer in its own order perhaps than ever before—is not enough. *It is not compelling the world; it is not even disturbing it; it scarcely comforts many who are actually looking to the Church for the inspiration they cannot find elsewhere.*

Why is this?

I believe it is because Christians appear to be no different from others in ordinary life, the life which others understand and with which they are familiar. What is "extraordinary" about them is not applied to what others feel to be extraordinary, or at least extraordinarily important.

It is an old accusation that Christians in time of war are found to be wholeheartedly fighting for different countries aiming at contrary ideals with important spiritual and moral import. And these same Christians remain indifferent to international and social reforms with high moral relevance. These may be superficial accusations against which there exists an adequate defence. But, whether this is so or not, we dare not underrate their immense importance. They go—I believe—a very long way towards accounting for the common indifference towards the Church. Christians, extraordinary in their own faith, appear to be very ordinary in their ability to divide themselves from one another in the pursuit of national ends, of conquest, of quasi-religious ideologies, and of uniting in indifference to peace, justice, and charity.

No doubt there is no easy or obvious answer. These rival causes, as I have said, are all mixtures of good and evil, and the Church as the Church cannot evade a difficulty by condemning the good with the bad, which would be the consequence of a general prohibition to all Catholics to participate in the struggles of the nations to which they belong. The answer is rather to be found in the long-standing failure of Christians themselves to pick their own way for themselves between the good and the evil, so that they gradually come to be known as men and women expected to take a stand in defence of their consciences, as men and women who, while participating in temporal affairs, always stand, as it were, over and above them. The Church, speaking for all, should light the way, while the individual acts, and in acting solves—well or ill—the practical Christian problem.

(iii) THE EXAMPLES OF CATHOLICS IN FRANCE

The beginnings of such a process of re-education to Christian action were perhaps to be found in the later days of the French Republic. Books were written that boldly set out the problems of the Christians in the face of contemporary philosophy and decadence. A positive, solid, forward-moving Christianity was taught and preached. Cardinals and bishops spoke out about the social problem, defending what was just in the workers' claims and denouncing what was unjust in national and individual capitalism. Above all, perhaps, Catholic Action in the great Jocist movement encouraged Catholics to be extraordinary in ordinary life, extraordinary not only in virtue, but extraordinary in mind and attitude. An enemy will say that this positive Catholicity was yet another factor making for national weakness and defeat. Exactly what influence this movement has had in subsequent French history is a matter for fascinating speculation, but it must be left to writers of the future who will know more of the facts and be able to see them in better perspective. But the Christian mind will not be deterred even if it can be shown to be a factor in accounting for defeat. To be so deterred is to confess that one is accepting as absolute and final those contemporary values that fall so far short of the Christian truth. That Christian movement, if maintained, may have heralded the birth of a new France—a France which, however, will grow to maturity only after many generations and through years of infinite suffering. The soul can be lost as well in victory as in defeat. And it can be saved in defeat as well as in victory.

(iv) THE CASE OF THE LATIN COUNTRIES

We may contrast with this the story of Christianity in Spain and Italy. It is acknowledged that in both countries

THE CHURCH IN ACTION   79

the spiritual life of the Church has been purified and strengthened. But it has paid a heavy price in accepting without opposition the ascendant political philosophy. We have, of course, to allow for a chequered past in which the Church was virtually outlawed as a factor of national importance—except where and when it could help the powers-that-were, but the degree of Catholic acceptance of a State order and policy in so many respects thoroughly non-Christian, and even completely amoral, has been anything but reassuring. And even if it were in itself defensible, given a full knowledge of the circumstances, we should still have to admit the degree of scandal caused elsewhere, and precisely in countries like Britain and America whose policies have counted so heavily in shaping the course of contemporary history.

But we must not run ahead too fast. The spiritual development of Catholicity in such countries is, whatever happens, an asset in itself. We cannot tell what is going on behind the scenes. But it may be—one has reason to believe it to be so—that the faithful, spiritually refreshed, are being trained to take a sturdier part in the changes which the future is likely to bring. However this be, one is surely right in suggesting that much depends upon this. In the churches, in the homes, men, women, and children must be trained to be a Christian *élite*, persons who can think for themselves, who can live and defend their Christian faith in those unforeseeable circumstances which affect nations and individuals. It may be that under the onslaught of anti-clerical liberalism, with its specious doctrine and its air of emancipation, the very spiritual quality of the Christian life was affected and that, as a consequence, the faithful were simply unprepared to see the dangers of a political revival which openly used the Church as a convenient instrument. Is the strengthening of the Church's position resulting in the training of

Christians who may not be able to affect the present order, but who can make a full Christian stand in the troubled times to come? That is the question. That is the test by which the world will judge the real worth of Christianity in great Catholic countries—and itself act accordingly.

We must also remember that in these Latin countries the moral problem sets itself in somewhat different terms from the ones to which we are accustomed in Anglo-Saxon countries. The Latins, with their strong Catholic tradition, attach far less importance to politics and international affairs, which they habitually regard as a game of trickery and force, and rather more importance to personal intellectual and cultural integrity. Personal, domestic, social, and cultural life is what really matters, and in this a man's spiritual outlook counts for a great deal. Public affairs are commonly thought of as a dirty business in which anticlericals and clericals seek to use their principles as instruments in gaining wealth or power or distinction. Nothing is more puzzling to the cynical Latin than the Anglo-Saxon persuasion that there can be a moral purpose, a Divine design, in the pursuit of national and international politics. But this Latin cynicism is already weakening. The great ideologies have been preached and propagated, and though they are accepted, even by their more fervent disciples, with a grain of salt, it has become impossible to maintain the dissociation between private and public life. The Latin Catholic cannot go on much longer imagining that his faith has little to do with his citizenship. And when he really does become alive to the situation he may surprise us Catholics of the north by the vigour of his reaction. A realist, he is likely to jump back to an earlier and simpler age and seek to conquer, not for anything so bloodless as international justice or the decencies of civilisation, but for Christ. Something of this spirit was undoubtedly manifested in the Spanish Civil War among the Requetes, to the great scandal of the English gentleman. But we can learn from it. And something of it was also manifested in the Basques, many of whom endured harsh criticism and condemnation for their adherence to a principle in which they believed. This clash between the Catholic Requetes and the Catholic Basques illustrates the truth that Christians in seeking to judge for themselves are not necessarily in agreement with each other. That is inevitably the result of human judgment, even within the one Church. But the world, so long as it becomes aware of the purpose to be Christian in action, is not necessarily scandalised by this. It is not looking for a mechanised formula, but for Christian living —a living which it can share.

(v) IN ANGLO-SAXON COUNTRIES

In Britain and America the Catholic finds himself in a very peculiar position. His trouble is that his Christian moral and social ideals appear to be so very inferior to those of his religiously indifferent countrymen. They crusade for progress, justice, the four freedoms, decency, the Wilsonian or the Atlantic Charter, the League of Nations, Federalism, business honesty, the maintenance of the pledged word, disarmament, the abolition of slavery, cruelty, aggression, barbarous methods of warfare, etc.; and the unfortunate Catholic, who finds it hard enough to lead a reasonably Christian life himself in a slick, hard, largely decadent pagan atmosphere, finds it terribly hard to keep up with all this super-Christian idealism. He cannot oppose such splendid idealism, yet he sometimes wonders how it is that the vast and wealthy Anglo-Saxon civilisation has in fact used its wealth and greatness and influence to so little good purpose, seeing that the world has steadily deteriorated in most of the above respects through its period of domination. He wonders, too, how it can be that the greater the loss of effective belief in God and Christianity in Britain and America, the higher are the moral ideals which they outwardly profess. A Christian country, unless it is actually fighting for the Faith as such, has some reluctance in proclaiming its national cause to be a crusade; but the Anglo-Saxon countries never take up the sword without being utterly persuaded that they are fighting God's battles.

It is small wonder, then, if the English or American Catholic, faced on the one side by Christian countries selling themselves to the Devil and on the other with the great indifferentist Anglo-Saxon world fighting for God, feels a little uncertain of himself and glad enough to be allowed to retire to his own spiritual shell, emerging as a plain Englishman or American. Those who try to make a public stand for Catholic values actually find it difficult to avoid appearing to advocate cruder and more material "foreign" ideals than are implied in the commonplace sentiments of politicians and Press.

Yet here also times are slowly changing. The gilt edge of Anglo-Saxon idealism is wearing thin, and what it covers is seen to be somewhat shoddy. But unfortunately it is not the Christian who has rubbed it away through concentrating upon the essentials of an order founded on the spiritual, moral, and economic rights and duties of the person, white, black, yellow, poor, rich, Latin, Anglo-Saxon, made in the image of God. It is not the Christian who has dwelt on the grossly unequal division of wealth and opportunity between nation and nation and man and man. It is not the Christian who has pointed out the irresponsible power heaped up into the hands of the big industrialist or financier, to whom the throwing of thousands upon thousands into unemployment is but an incident of business life that the country cannot *afford* to remedy. It is not the Christian who has shown up the hollow pretence of trying to dictate to the world a moral code in which the maintenance of the comfortable *status quo* is hallowed with every sanctimonious epithet, while the people's morals and morale are allowed to decay through the application of the sole law of supply and demand to the very stuff which makes or breaks a man's life and character. It is not the Christian who has protested against the absurdity of maintaining the great supplies of the world's raw materials while raising tariffs which make it impossible for less fortunate countries even to purchase those materials. All these protests in the last years of the old regime have come in their force, not from the Christian, but from the Socialist. The Socialist has not been afraid of courting national unpopularity and social ostracism by criticising to the roots the structure of Anglo-Saxon capitalism. And that is why we must expect the Socialist to become a power to-morrow.

But the Socialist has at bottom no solution except to extend, first to the State and then to the whole world, the particularist vices of capitalism with more than a touch of the Bolshevist or Nazist totalitarianism thrown in. Not a handful of persons, not a handful of nations, but mechanised civilisation itself, armed by every weapon of science and propaganda, will impose mass production, mass pleasures, mass culture, mass dodging of reality, mass moral sentiment, mass employment (or mass unemployment) upon all peoples. In the full socialist era it will be easy to monopolise every religious formula and every moral qualification, since there will be no opposition. To the Christian-inherited ideals of justice and freedom even lip-service may no longer be paid.

Is it really necessary for the Christian to keep silent? Is he not capable, on the basis of his faith, whose teaching and inspiration extend over all creation, polarised, as it were, by God above and the person of each and every man below, of speaking his mind? And is he not capable of acting in accordance with a Christian judgment? But if the Christian, whether Catholic or Anglican, is so overwhelmed by the nobility and moral superiority of Anglo-Saxondom, how can we possibly expect others to interest themselves in what Christianity has to contribute?

But nowhere is the tradition of keeping silence and minding our own religious business more strongly entrenched than in this country. Does not the British rule protect the Church both in England and the Empire? How much we have to lose by unpopularity! How little apparently to gain! That is the substance of what we are taught, and it is constantly reinforced by reminders of how right Britain is and how wrong her enemies and rivals. Of course there is much truth in this, but if we put our trust in it too far, if we make it our habit of mind, we are in effect saying that the Christian spirit fulfils itself as far as temporal matters are concerned in the British outlook and practice. If this is the case why should non-Christians look to the Church? Yet many, in the visible caving-in of the past and the uncertainties and dangers of the future, are looking wistfully to a Christian solution. Are we content to hand back to them the very outlook from which they seek to escape?

(vi) IS QUALITY SACRIFICED TO QUANTITY AND SAFETY?

Looking, finally, to the work of Christianity across the face of the globe, to what ends are the greatest Christian effort and work directed? Probably to the work of bringing the Sacraments to those who live their lives on the very edge of Catholic practice. It has been said that the work of the Church in its relation with temporal powers can best be understood if we remember that the Church's object is to be in a position to bring the last Sacraments to as many souls as possible. This means in effect that the first work of the Church is to secure the largest quantity of at least death-bed Catholics. To this the world might answer: but surely God, Who founded the Church, and Whose grace is canalised through the Church, can make up for the reasonable inability of the Church to be within call of everyone? Surely the Church should concentrate on being the witness to the full truth in daily life and on helping as many as possible to rise as high as possible; for these things God, by revealing Truth to the Church and by making her the channel of grace, has willed her to do. Meanwhile God himself is not likely to fail to give such direct help as is necessary to souls who, through no fault of their own or of the Church, remain outside the visible fold. Is it not possible to sacrifice some quantity to higher quality? And might it not even be the case that the pursuit of quantity actually defeats its own object? Might not better quality among fewer result in the conversion of more?

How much work and effort are expended in teaching and training Catholics to be Catholics in mind and action in their weekday lives, in their citizenship, in their business, in their avocations? How can Catholics learn to be extraordinary in their ordinary affairs? And here too might it not with justice be suggested that, at a time when the world needs the Church as never before, when it often looks to the Church, but when it is separated from the extraordinary in the Church as never before, both quality and quantity could rapidly be improved by Catholics demonstrating the quality, meaning, and practical effects of the mysterious faith which vivifies them? At any rate, if we look to the methods of other successful educators, to the Jews, to the Fascists, to the Nazis, to the British public school, we shall find there little hesitation in tackling the problem of how to make a man a Jew, a Fascist, a Nazi, an Englishman, not in the privacy of his own home alone, but in every act, thought, and breath of life. You do not first hear of Nazism through reading *Mein Kampf* or visiting the Brown House in Munich. "Action," as the scholastics put it, "follows being."

(vii) CHARACTERISTICS OF THE REVOLUTION AROUND US—GERMANY

So much for the past. More important is it to consider the future. Unfortunately there is no telling the nature of that future—not even in the groping, halting way of more normal times. The War, like a storm, has tossed and mingled the relatively stable factors of the old world, and the mighty currents that run beneath the surface commotion and the war-directed currents are still indiscernible. But we may be sure the world will not settle down to a peaceful order of itself. It failed to do so after the last war, and the Second World War is the consequence of the failure to settle by intelligent and morally based control the world that emerged from four years of war.

To-day we face a Europe—indeed a world—whose peoples are seething with keen aspirations of diverse and contrary kinds, quasi-religious aspirations, cultural aspirations, political aspirations—most of them artificially repressed during war itself—and, above all, social and economic aspirations. Hitler, with the aid of the German nationalistic sentiments and the most powerful military and political machine of all time, has attempted to satisfy some of the strongest of those aspirations, notably the social and economic ones, by imposing a dictatorial order. His idea, at its best, seems to have been ruthlessly to suppress all those aspirations which do not seem to him to serve the purpose of making Europe a strong political and economic unity, and to foster what may be called the *socialistic* aspirations. By those I mean the aspirations towards economic security for the individual in an effectively organised and ultra-modern State commanding all the resources of modern science, industry, and technique. One trembles to think of what Hitler might have achieved in this way had not one side of his character been dominated by the short-sightedness, grossness, and brutality too often characteristic of the German. Even Churchill feared he might prove a new Charlemagne! But the nationalistic as opposed to the socialistic side of his character and movement has led him into the contradiction of attempting to satisfy Europe's socialist aspirations on the basis of first satisfying German's "Luxury" nationalist ones. The primitive idea of the German master race, the out-of-date notion that one country can be suzerain and all others mere vassals, has played into the hands of his enemies inside and outside Europe, has prolonged the War, and made our victory possible.

But in his socialist aims Hitler was on the practical track. And even Hitler's present achievements in effecting a rough war-time political and economic unity for Europe will probably make it impossible for the Continent to return to the old divisions and competitions. The more so in that Hitler was but one instrument of forces making for a new economic order in an ethos wherein the moral principles of liberty and justice, founded on Christian reason, tradition, and dogma, were rapidly weakening.

(viii) THE INEVITABLE CONSEQUENCES ON EUROPE

Hitler has treated Europe as a brutal but intelligent master might treat his servants. Gaining control of them as dissatisfied and quarrelling human beings, such a master might by bribes, fear, and psychological tricks condition them into being his instruments in a common enterprise wherein they could not but feel an essential satisfaction.

They would, however, never lose their hatred for the master who could hypnotise them into doing his will, who could convert them outwardly into his creatures. But with the fall of their master they could not recover for many years, and without the most skilful treatment, their former independence and self-sufficiency. Unless someone else could be found to do their willing for them, they would be in danger of perishing through sheer ineffectiveness, lack of means, and childish indulgence in passions so long forcibly restrained.

But the analogy hopelessly fails to do justice to the complexity of the situation where it is a question of nations and not of men. The economy of each of these conquered or dominated countries has been twisted and forced into new channels, while being heavily strained for the un-economic purposes of war. The international trade on which they all depend to some extent has been destroyed, the very ships which cross the ocean having been sunk. Many countries have been divided into two parties, some people siding with what they consider to be the cause of order, unity, prosperity, and security—and those we call the "quislings"—while others put first nation, freedom, and, in some cases, the hope at a later date of a workers' international. Religious beliefs add to the chaos, for some hold that religion demands resistance to persecuting totalitarianism and others fear the social anarchy that might follow the overthrow of the Nazis and Fascists by Powers that are anti-clerical, masonic, philo-communist, what-not. So that numberless internal stresses and strains are at work within each nation drawn under the Hitlerian domination by force and hypnotic suggestion. And these stresses and strains, be it noted, are not the effect of some political game or other, some self-seeking economic interest; they spring from the very hearts of the people themselves. We must never forget that we are not dealing now with countries retaining a traditional and inherited order that remains proof against even violent political changes, as in the past; we are dealing with masses of peoples educated to take an intimate personal interest in their conditions of life, incessantly flattered by politicians, believing themselves to possess the right to determine their own economic and political future. Even Nazism, Fascism, and Bolshevism have been forced to respect these convictions of the half-educated emancipated masses of the mid-twentieth century. Their technique of despotism is throughout "popular"! Half the energy and ingenuity of the leaders is directed to convincing the people that they are acting in their name and for them, that they are expressing *their* will. The Secret Police and the armies alone cannot maintain power to-day. Just as important is that technique of modern propaganda, whose job it is to persuade the governed that they are the real governors. Hence everywhere, in the Fascist and Bolshevist countries just as much as in the free or temporarily conquered countries, we are face to face with this in itself unformed, but dynamic and often desperate, bid for political and economic self-expression on the part of millions. And it is these millions of whom some are persuaded for the time being that their hope lies in the new totalitarian State, and others, on the contrary, fight for ideals that seem to them to be contrary to those of the conqueror. The older instruments of restraint and order, whether principles of religion or the historical inheritance in the shape of separate autonomous countries with their own political system, laws, and customs, have been destroyed throughout most of Europe and replaced by this great, central, hypnotic, tyrannic, yet "popular," economically interested Power. Let it be removed by external force and what will happen? Unless something can replace it, and immediately, there can be nothing but the clash of a million lost but intensely alive wills, each seeking for some part or other of the confused ideal of order, economic security, freedom, national loyalty, religious or ideological allegiance—and each seeking for this in a state of complete political confusion and intense poverty, amounting in many cases to near or absolute starvation. Something like a minor dress rehearsal of the post-War stresses and strains has already been enacted among Frenchmen freed from German domination. It augurs ill for the future.

(ix) THE NATURE OF THE CONTROL TO BE EXERCISED BY THE VICTORS

It is difficult to see, under the conditions which will obtain in Europe, and to some extent throughout the world, after this war, how international and national order will be possible short of the immediate organisation of a centrally directed economic—and largely political—control by the victor Powers. This will be necessary, if for no other reason, in order to avoid sheer anarchy and famine. But what complexion will this control have? To what will it lead? It is impossible to foresee this in detail. At least it is evident that the task of reorganising Europe, in the state in which it will find itself after war, so that the immediate economic needs of all men may be met, and man's status gradually improved, cannot be less difficult than the task of finding the economic resources to wage war. Indeed it will be much more difficult, if only because the artificial spirit of self-sacrifice and co-operation which war engenders will have disappeared. Its place will be taken by a million emancipated wills struggling in almost as many directions, and generally for themselves in the first place. The old national divisions, the old autonomies, crowns, and constitutions, the old cultural and legal rights, may or may not remain outwardly the same, but unless they in fact yield to this supernational or international economic control there can be little hope of avoiding anarchy, and none of gradually recovering efficiency and prosperity.

Is it not likely that this control will develop along totalitarian lines, the lines of what is perhaps best described as Marxism—Marxism, the rule of the *impersonal*, the real rival to Christian principles, which on the contrary are based upon the self-rule of the *person*?

I do not mean by Marxism the out-of-date economic theories of Karl Marx, but rather his material philosophic presuppositions and the ideal of a "brave new world" emerging from strain and conflict—the idea of international powers, claiming to represent the will of the masses for social and economic security and, if possible, equality, controlling all resources (including of course all human energy) for the purpose of creating a paradise on earth, according to the prescriptions of the scientists, popular philosophers, and technicians. I repeat that, as regards the essence of the business, it will not greatly matter what precise outward shape this master idea may take, though one form may be much more comfortable than another. Had Germany defeated us it would have taken a Nazi shape, that is, the power would have been openly exercised by the Nazi party in the immediate interests of the German race; but if such a conquering Nazism were to survive at all it could only have been through serving the economic needs and the social demands of the masses in Europe and to some extent outside Europe. When we win—and if we do not allow Europe to sink into chaos—the old forms may be to some extent outwardly preserved, but we, in conjunction with America and Russia, will be forced to impose, either directly or, more probably, through national governments, this Machine which, if cleverly and unscrupulously propagated in terms of Marxism, would arouse the support of the European masses.

Prophesying is considered the most gratuitous way of making a fool of oneself, but I am not prophesying that all this *will* happen. It is, I fear, even more likely that we shall have to endure a long period of deep disorder, confusion, economic misery, civil wars and revolts, with individual nations making impossible and hopeless attempts to restore some degree of internal order and economic health, aided, no doubt, by the ineffective good-will of a powerless international machinery. All I am saying is that the one practical chance, given the present state of men's minds, of recovering from the War and building a new Europe lies along these international lines. Whoever retains actual authority and force after the War will have to take the initiative boldly and quickly, assuming and enforcing a well-nigh universal economic control of this nature. What the actual chances of this happening are I cannot say. The desperate need may create the required will.

(x) AN UGLY PICTURE WE MUST FACE

By this time, readers, especially Catholic readers, will be aghast at the complacency with which I suggest, and even apparently recommend, the inevitable triumph—unless indeed we revert to a new Dark Age—of everything which they and I consider most abhorrent. But Christians will do themselves no good by refusing to face foreseeable dangers or trying to blind themselves to truths because such truths seem inconvenient, or inconsistent with their own too-wishful thinking. There exists a type of Christian who piously imagines that the opponent of Christianity must necessarily fail, not merely in terms of Christian values, but in terms of pagan or secularist values. He is convinced that Fascists and Bolsheviks and Nazis must be not only bad Christians, but bad Fascists, Bolsheviks, and Nazis.

He is appalled to discover that pagans can fight, keep order, enforce natural virtues essential to the stability of the State, create temporal prosperity. In allowing such temporal triumphs God, he begins to fear, has deserted the good cause. Yet what could be more natural than that worldly success should come to those who are intelligent and strong enough to seek worldly ends? The prosperity of the wicked is as old as the world, and it is often obtained through the thoughtless services of the honest and sincere servants of the wicked.

It is very possible that the world must work its way right through all the stages of the experiment of doing without God and trying to replace Him by man. And the next step would seem to be the creation of this mighty "Machine," ruthlessly and efficiently destroying men for man's sake, and creating an earthly paradise which no one may enjoy. It may be, I repeat, that the effort to reach this stage will not be forthcoming and that the disintegration due to thirty years of war and disorder has gone too far to allow of recovery even along these totalitarian lines. In that case we have only a long period of anarchy to which to look forward.

No wonder that, under these circumstances, the hopes of many are concentrated on Christianity, as the last international force capable of tempering the new totalitarianism or the one discipline capable of seeing man through an era of anarchy, a new Dark Age. We are living in a period of extreme tension—tension between good and evil, tension between the good in the service of evil and evil—or at least stupidity—in the service of good. In such a period something in the nature of a spiritual explosion always remains possible. A sudden wind from Heaven could open men's eyes to the truth and in a very short period a spiritual revolution at the price of intense suffering—something of the kind *may* be taking place in France—could occur. Such, I suggest, are the conditions for which Christians themselves should be preparing.

(xi) THE RÔLE OF RELIGION

In considering the part that Christianity could play in this new world we must be on our guard against misunderstanding the rôle of religion.

Christianity is concerned with ends, the ends in fact which tend to make men more like God as He revealed himself to be, more fully to God's "image and likeness"; it is not so nearly concerned with means. Christianity teaches that you ought to want A and strive towards A; it does not teach us so clearly that if you want A *you must do B*. Both personal and social life form an extremely complex hierarchy of means leading to ends, these ends in their turn becoming means to higher and wider ends, and so on, the whole complex structure making for a supreme end. In practice of course the plan is always more or less incomplete, for we move ahead into a thickening fog in which our ends are only dimly perceived, and, too often, in contradiction with one another. But the Christian revelation teaches clearly the supreme end as well as many lesser ends, so that the general nature of the design which we should follow can be apprehended. But it does not reveal the infinite number and variety of means which in their turn become ends. At the most it makes clear that certain means and certain ends are running clean counter to the true design. It tells us, in other words, what character and quality of life we should pursue, and it warns us against pursuing a course that must be incompatible with this pursuit. It does not reveal at any given moment what in fact we should be doing in order to achieve our true ends. That is a matter of trial and error, ingenuity, study, training, experience, technique, and, above all, good

habits.   Christianity cannot replace the State and other
institutions.   Christianity in itself does not solve technical
problems, whether of science or art, of politics or economics.
So that if one day you turn to the Christian revelation in
order to find out how the modern world can be saved from
the disastrous consequences of its past mistakes you will
find no ready answer.   And this is an extremely important
point, for that in fact is what many who hanker after a
Christian solution expect.   They seem to imagine that
because one loves one's neighbour, or decides to live by
the counsels of the Sermon on the Mount, or even to become
a Catholic, one will also be given pat solutions to the social
political, economic, and technical problems of the day.
But being a Christian in no way exempts one from the need
to think and study and experiment and make one's own
choices and decisions.   Must we then, it may be asked,
cease to look to Christianity for practical guidance in a
critical situation like the present?   The only possible answer
is "yes and no."

Where Christianity is practised, where it·gives shape
and meaning and inspiration to life, whether personal or
national, one can rightly expect practical and technical help
from Christianity.   For what does this mean?   It means
that the person or nation concerned has been trying to
solve his technical problems *within the general pattern of life
furnished by the Christian revelation*.   In other words, they
have been keeping the *right end* in sight, they have been all
the time guided by the lighthouse of the faith.   Furthermore—to keep the metaphor—they have enjoyed the use
of a chart which plainly indicates many dangerous rocks
and shoals.   They know where they are going and they
know the chief perils to avoid.   It stands to reason that
their perfectly natural studies and experiments will under
such conditions prove more fruitful, more consistent with
the pattern.   And thus in course of time they will build

up a sound and useful technique of life. And it is in that sense and under such conditions that Christianity can be a guide, not only to the specifically religious and moral life, but to the practical life of politics and economics. Where Christianity is lived through society, day in and day out, a practical order that can be called Christian, because it subserves the true ends of man and society, comes into existence. In that sense, then, the answer to the question is "yes." But Christianity cannot be a short-cut to the practical solution of immensely difficult political and social problems that have arisen largely through the rejection of Christianity through the centuries. Still less can it be narrowed to the compass of any one of the fashionable ideologies. On the other hand it can go far towards making any of them healthy and hopeful by remedying their errors.

(xii) CHRISTIANITY'S REAL TASK

We can understand now that any contemporary appeal to Christianity as a mere escape from our difficulties cannot in itself have any great significance. The task before Christianity is rather (1) to prevent the development of any social order of its nature incompatible with Christian moral values, and (2) to see that whatever social order emerges, if it is at all compatible with Christianity, shall be Christian through its ends and rendered as little non-Christian as may be in its means. Even the emergence of the Machine is not necessarily incompatible with Christianity. A Machine is, of its nature, a machine to effect something. It is on that *something* that we should concentrate rather than on seeking to break up the Machine. The ends put forward in the Pope's 1942 Christmas Allocution, together with such means as are necessary to the attaining of these ends, are not incompatible with the degree of socialised planning that our present economic and social circumstances seem to make inevitable.   But it can scarcely be denied that the Machine, given its strength, its all-embracing action, and the materialist standardised quality which it gives to whatever it produces (and men themselves are in part its production), makes it very necessary indeed that Christianity seeks to be equally strong and all-embracing, equally concerned with any and every aspect of day-to-day life, international, national, social, personal, economic, if it is to carry the weight needed to make possible a restoration of Christian values in planned society.

Men (including nominal Christians leading double lives of Sunday religion and weekday paganism) must become Christians again, whole-time, full-hearted Christians, whose values are expressed as much in the market-place as in the cell, and in sufficient numbers, if the spiritual force of Christianity is to become powerful enough to set the world again on the task of constructing a new Christian order under such conditions.   There must be a coming together again of a disillusioned world to a living Church and of a living society of whole-time Christians to a world looking for a way of life, at least as deep and intense as its own, but ordered to right, and not self-contradictory, ends.

CHAPTER V

SOME PRACTICAL POINTS OF REFORM

(i) QUALIFICATIONS FOR MAKING CERTAIN SUGGESTIONS

At this stage it might be expected of me to suggest concrete lines of reform and change which could help to fit Christianity for the tremendous task with which it will be faced after the War, if it is to interest, impress, and help a shattered world.

In a previous book [1] I said as much as I thought fit for the pen of an irresponsible layman.   It is one thing to try to work out certain general implications about the functions of Christianity in its relation with the world, leaving it to those who are in positions of authority to consider what is put forward; it is quite another to pretend to tell them what they should be doing about it all.   Moreover my main concern in these pages has been with the position and responsibilities of the individual Catholic (like myself) who —if I am right—must always be the "monstrance" of Christianity.   There is really not much difficulty in living daily Christian lives—in applying the *extraordinary* in our Faith to ordinary circumstances and problems, if we have the will to do so—and no reform can save us from making that personal effort.   Still certain simple points, applying more particularly to my own country and arising from my own experience, may be made.   That experience is as editor of a weekly Catholic newspaper.   That newspaper (*The Catholic Herald*) has attempted during the last few years to put before British Catholics something of the ideal of personal action and responsibility under Catholic authority, as described in these pages.   We have necessarily moved cautiously, because much more harm than good is done by offering food that is too strong for the average digestion—and popular newspapers must inevitably cater in the main for those whose digestion in these matters is not particularly strong.   None the less, we should not have done our job if we had refused to run risks and say what we thought when the occasion arose.   Yet I can witness to the fact that in these years no single bishop has taken us to task, and only very occasionally has any suggested that things might have been better put.   On the contrary, we have received nothing but encouragement and help from the highest ecclesiastical quarters, and if advice

[1] *Christian Crisis* (Burns & Oates).

has been sought or offered it has always come in terms of
the fullest sympathy with our work. Quite frankly I have
been surprised at this, since Catholic newspapers must
inevitably have considerable influence on the minds of
Catholics as a whole, and mistakes, errors of judgment,
tactlessness are bound to be frequent if only because of the
speed with which work has to be done. Week by week
they are widely read; they are bound to cover many subjects
which intimately affect the interests of the Church, and
these they must cover very inadequately and with far too
little reflection.

I take this then as a living testimonial, not to the merits
or demerits of this particular paper, but to the truth that
the higher ecclesiastical authorities are extremely anxious
for lay Catholic initiative, so long as they themselves are
reasonably satisfied that that initiative is taken with a
sufficient understanding of Catholic authority and teaching,
with the right intentions, and with some judgment and
common sense. And if this is the case among Catholics,
how much more so in other communions!

But these conditions are of the utmost importance, and
they suggest the basic Catholic need in this country and
in every other: the need of proper instruction. A newspaper is in an exceptionally favourable position. It depends
upon the work of very few people, and it would be a tragedy
indeed if properly instructed Catholics with some judgment
and common sense were not available for the job. There
is no comparable Catholic activity. The work of societies,
organisations, and still more of individual Catholics in
their citizenship and business life, depends not upon the
proper instruction and sound judgment of two or three
people, acting on the minds of thousands, but upon
thousands, each acting on comparatively few others. And
proper instruction and training for the Catholic body in
general are necessary if a sufficiency of reliable workers is to

be obtained.   In this respect we are in a kind of vicious circle.   If the ecclesiastical authorities were satisfied about the instruction and judgment of Catholics as a whole, they would be far more willing to leave them unhampered in their different works; on the other hand, the present need for control and supervision and "safety first" makes it much more difficult to train men and women with real courage, initiative, and zeal.

Let me suggest, however—though with some diffidence —three places where this vicious circle can be broken. *Mutatis mutandis*, my suggestions can be applied to other Christian communions.

(ii) THE FIRST IS EDUCATION

The first and by far the most important is in our schools, elementary and secondary.   I have dealt with this at greater length in *Christian Crisis*, and much the same points have been recently put forward in articles and papers.

The traditional attempt to educate along two lines, a secular line *and* a religious line, just does not work.   It flatly contradicts all sound pedagogical principles, and it results in creating a permanent division in the mind of the child.   From it we get a minority of extraordinarily devout Catholics, who are extraordinarily ordinary in their civic and business life, and a majority who are extraordinary neither in their religious nor their secular lives.   The contrast with the effects of an integrated education, as given to Jews, Fascists, and ordinary citizens who reflect the contemporary national-secularist philosophy, is painful. Whatever the cost, Catholics must be educated from the beginning to understand and live everything in terms of the teaching, philosophy, and practice of Christianity.   This does *not* mean that all Catholics must be trained to be *religious*.   When we jump to this conclusion we are simply falling victims to the old fallacy of separating religious from secular.   There is nothing *religious* about history, mathematics, science, business training, and the like.   These things, like every other weekday Catholic activity, must remain secular throughout.   But they must also be Catholic, *i.e.* they must find their appropriate place within God's unified and meaning-full pattern.   Addition and subtraction do not change in themselves, whether they are taught by an atheist or a Catholic saint; but the atheist, even if unconsciously, will teach them as evidence of his philosophy and as potential instruments in the building of a world "which has no need of that hypothesis, God," while the Catholic will teach them as part of the Divine Order to be used in the service of God's plan.   Indeed where could be found a better opportunity of revealing to the child the height and depth and width of Catholicity, as God's plan, than in the school curriculum?   Yet our Catholic education appears to be generally organised in terms of nine-tenths ordinary text-book with secularist values and one-tenth almost wholly unrelated religious instruction and devotion! It is not surprising—as many have found in practice—that the Catholic child with a good Catholic home sometimes actually fares better as a Catholic in a non-Catholic school. For in a non-Catholic environment the contrast between home and school forces the child to think for itself, and to build up its own Catholic outlook in opposition to the school's secularist outlook.   Too often in the Catholic school it is imbibing secularism under the impression that it is Christianity.

It is in the earliest years that a child forms its moral habit of mind, and it is therefore from the earliest years that the Catholic outlook in regard not only to personal morality but to the values of newspaper, fiction, text-book, grown-up conversation, history, geography, science, etc., must be formed.   What can we expect from a training which—outside personal morality—allows the contemporary values of the world to seep in, and then is content with a few lessons or sermons just before leaving school to repair the damage done?

Nor should the training be negative. We get negative training when individual schoolmasters, mistresses, parents, and priests feel it to be their duty to tell the child, every so often, that this and this and this are wrong or inaccurate. Unless they are prepared to accept the whole secularist bag of tricks they are bound to do this. But if the training from the beginning were positively Christian, and Catholic, there would be far less need of these confusing correctives. The child, from the beginning, would see life in a Christian perspective. It would learn to appreciate the true order. It would become intensely proud of it. It would leave school as keen on Christian apostolate in the widest sense as any young Hitlerite or Stalinite is keen on living and preaching the false gospel taught him.

Unfortunately this is the slow method, and there is an increasing danger that the school education of many Christians will be taken out of religious hands. Strangely enough perhaps, after what I have said, I do not believe that such a loss need prove fatal. The difficulties of providing a full Christian education under a State education system are so great that there is something to be said for exploring alternative means. The Christian child who knows from the beginning that he is to be taught his lessons in an environment that is hostile to his own faith will not be in danger of confusing all that is taught and happens in a so-called Catholic school with Christianity. Under secularist education we may lose a number of Catholics who would otherwise have remained outwardly Catholic, but we might well gain tremendously through the better instruction and greater toughness of the rest. I am not indeed advocating the jettisoning of our Catholic schools, for the risk involved in that *under present conditions* would be appalling. But I suggest that if we do in the end lose them, it will be possible so adequately to compensate for the loss that we may not lose in the end, but perhaps actually gain. We must certainly fight for our schools, but I venture to suggest that there is something lopsided in the activity of Catholics on the schools question as compared with other possible fields of action. If we paid equal attention to self-reform, and to reform of Catholic institutions and movements, the schools question might not be so important. Our aim is Catholic education of children and youth, and an over-reliance on the present very unsatisfactory educational system (in which the demands of the world carry so much weight, and, very often, are allowed to do so under Catholic auspices) may actually result in a worse Catholic education (*i.e.* an education, spiritual and secular, in the light of Christian values) than an avowed secularist schooling counterbalanced by real Catholic training elsewhere. This brings me to the second place where the vicious circle can be broken, namely the parish, and the family.

(iii) THE PARISH AND THE FAMILY

It is still, thank God, the case that the great majority of Catholics go to church at least once a week. They should not be allowed to leave it without getting some plain words about their responsibilities as Catholics and some advice about what they ought to be doing. The first interest of the clergy is very naturally to strengthen the spiritual life of their people. But I suggest—with all deference—that the time has come when the need for the strengthening of what I am bold enough to call the Catholic daily life of the people is just as vital. I should even like to suggest that the devotional life of people and parish will be most effectively strengthened if the faithful are regularly reminded of what it means to be a Catholic in the contemporary world of 1943. Imagine the effect of a sermon in which the preacher took into the pulpit that Sunday morning's issue of a mammoth-sale national newspaper. Imagine him reading out passages, and pointing out the clash between the values in politics, economics, social questions, entertainment, etc., taken for granted in that paper, and the values which the Catholic should be living and furthering! Would not a congregation so treated begin to sit up and take notice? Would not its dormant faith be suddenly galvanised into full life? And that is only one example of hundreds of possible methods of giving live instruction. Is the clergy equal to this, it may be asked. Of course it is, but how much more could be done if the training in seminaries and colleges envisaged this kind of modern apostolate.

The parish moreover gives the opportunity for the specialised training of a keen minority which, if the methods used were sound and inspiring, would soon become a majority. And this is where the laity's energy and talents can be given full scope. As far as I understand the matter, I should say that the general principles and technique of the Y.C.W.[1] give us the best model. These points, I suggest, should be kept in mind: (1) The appeal should not be exclusively to the pious—the "sacristified," to use Fr. Rochford's brilliant term. The appeal should be to those who want to use their *brains*, to those who want to be up and doing *something* to make more sense of their lives. (2) The priest's function in this field should be exclusively that of chaplain and adviser; and these rôles should be exercised in the broadest and most sympathetic

---

[1] Y.C.W. means Young Christian Workers, the English branch of the international J.O.C. (Jeunesse Ouvrière Catholique). It has also spread to the Anglican communion.

spirit possible.   As lay activity develops and finds its own feet, so the priest will find it less and less necessary to interfere, though in fact it will often happen that his help and advice will be more and more required.   In other words, a natural relationship between two separate but interdependent functions will be created.   (3) The purpose throughout is not to achieve anything directly, least of all successful whist drives and dances; it is instruction and, above all, self-instruction by mutual contact, discussion, and common study.

And the subject throughout is simply "what is involved in being a Christian in this country, in this town or village, in this year of the Lord."   Action in plenty will spring from the obtaining of clear and convinced ideas on this subject, action in business life, in one's profession, in the factory, in the home, in the pub, and everywhere else.   At the same time it would of course be well if definite parish needs in the way of social help, youth training, distribution of literature, visiting the poor, contacting non-Catholics for common civic enterprise and the like can be organised, as the Legion of Mary does.   But it would be a pity if the work of creation of Catholic minds were swamped by such preoccupations and the business and difficulties attached to them.   (4) Lastly, I personally would suggest—though few will follow me here—that less stress should be laid on common devotional exercises, monthly communions, and the like.   If the work is alive and prospers, a full devotional life for each member will automatically result, and it seems to me better and more natural that it should express itself by a more fervent personal participation in the ordinary parish devotions than in specialised ones.   Above all it is important not to drive away the less "pious," through suggesting that the "last-Sunday-Mass" Catholic is not wanted.   He is badly wanted—wanted, indeed, more than others.

4*

The parish should develop into the Christian cell, and every family in the parish should feel organically one with every other so that a dynamic community, sensitively reacting to secularist environment, is formed. The liturgy, instruction, Catholic training, Christian life, under priestly and lay leadership, are its natural sphere of action. The Catholic individual (from babyhood to old age) is the person - in - Catholic - family, and the Catholic family the family - in - Catholic - parish. There is the final answer to the school problem! The difficulties in the way, I know, are tremendous. Lack of clergy, lack of initiative and imagination in priests and laity, geographical difficulties, lack of time, arrant stupidity in so many, lack of funds to build the kind of structure that could centre Catholic social life, as the Church centres religious life, the danger of forming a closed corporation and consequent insularity— but these difficulties can be overcome, and I can think of no line of reform that would more rapidly and thoroughly make Catholics *extraordinary* in ordinary life than the creation of the real parish cell.

(iv) CATHOLIC ORGANISATION THROUGHOUT THE COUNTRY

The last place where the vicious circle can be broken is in diocesan, national, and international organisation. This is a much wider and much more difficult subject, and I shall content myself with throwing out a few ideas.

The great danger of all Catholic organisation—outside the exclusively ecclesiastical province, of course—is the creation of something approaching a theocracy. It would not in theory be difficult to work out a scheme of Catholic Action by which all fervent Catholics would find themselves organised, according to their professions or interests, in a system of guilds under episcopal direction. But the natural effect of such a scheme would be still further to separate Catholic life and interests from the world. Moreover it would almost certainly leave out of its membership thousands who ought to be within it. It would appeal to the already fervent, to those who want to be extraordinary in their devotional life, but of whom there is no guarantee that they either are or want to be extraordinary in their weekday life as Catholic men of the world.

To avoid this danger, we must look less to what one might call the "professional" Catholics (those whose names habitually appear on Catholic committees) and more to those Catholics who, whatever their present professional Catholic interest, have shown their capacity by their careers. We must turn to successful business men, to higher officers in the Services, to civil and diplomatic servants, to lawyers, to doctors, to writers, to trade-union leaders, to members of parliament, to members of municipalities, to university professors, to artists, to scientists. And in the same way we must pick out from factories, farms, shops the men and women of character and leadership. And to all of these we must offer something that will *excite* them.

It will be objected that many of these have nothing but a "Sunday" interest in their religion—if that—and are quite uninstructed in the very points about which I am writing. That may be the case, but in most cases it is in no way their own fault. And the very fact that they have shown ability and character in their respective walks of life makes it very likely that they will quickly come to appreciate the ideal of a living, integrated Christian outlook such as we have in mind, especially when the approach is intellectual and not merely devotional and ecclesiastical. Their independence of outlook and their experience, moreover, will prove precious guarantees against the "sacristification" and theocratic tendencies of Catholic organisations. Somehow the whole social action of the

Church (*i.e.* of Christians within the Church and members of Christ's Mystical Body) must be broadened and made more serious. At present it can only be called, from top to bottom, narrow, provincial, petty. We cannot be content with a social action that falls short of the heights, depths, and seriousness of our worship.

I can visualise a broadly conceived Catholic organisation working on four planes. One plane is the plane of the clergy, whose duty is spiritual and instructional. The next plane is what may be called an academic plane. On this plane clergy and laity would work together, thinking out principles of action, trying to apply Christian teaching and tradition—and not least the inspiration of the great social and political encyclicals—to concrete problems—a kind of Catholic "brains trust" recruited from seminaries, universities, professional experts, writers, artists, etc. A third plane would be a plane of actual leadership recruited from the types mentioned in the previous paragraph, men of the world and experience, who thoroughly understand conditions of work and life. And the last plane would be the plane of co-workers and ordinary membership from every station in life.

Into these horizontal divisions could be fitted the vertical professional organisations of doctors, lawyers, business, services, industry, and so on.

Out of all this would come a broad Catholic front, at work in and within the world, designed in the first instance to help every individual Catholic to be a living Catholic in his particular life and position, and, in the second instance, to represent and defend Catholic and Christian truth and values at all points in the national life in the most natural and spontaneous way according to the circumstances.

The chief advantage of a loosely knit, yet comprehensive and well-led Catholic front of this kind would be that in it could be reconciled three stages or functions of Catholic

Action.   First and foremost the position of the individual Catholic would be strengthened.   He would feel himself to be a living focus of the spiritual and secular which together make up his Catholicity; and his life could become a life of balanced Catholic Action in accordance with his own judgment, capacity, and tastes.   Nor would he find any difficulty in co-operation with the world, with other Christians, with his trade union, party, etc., where such co-operation is necessary and desirable.   But all the time he would be capable of judging, and willing to judge, as an instructed and supported Catholic, proud of this greater loyalty.   Secondly those Catholic men and women, determined and prepared to go furthest in the defence within the world of Christian spiritual and moral values, could be developed in relation with the rest of the faithful.   They would constitute a kind of vanguard, yet avoid the present danger of being looked upon as, and consequently sometimes becoming, cranks, or *punaises de sacristie*, as the French call it.   And thirdly national Catholicity as a whole would be in action all along the front in flexible and ever-changing ways, according to the needs of the moment and the method best adapted under particular circumstances for success. And I do not see why something of all this should not obtain in the other Christian communions who to-day stand as comparatively small and apathetic minorities in a secularised nation.

(v) CO-OPERATION BETWEEN CATHOLICS AND NON-CATHOLICS—A NEW WAY

This leads me to the all-important question of co-operation with non-Catholics.   It is only too evident that the Christian counterweight to the secularism of the world must be made up of as many recruits as possible.   Those who have followed me so far, and noted the insistence on the need for *extraordinary* Christianity in ordinary affairs, may be ready to agree that that *extraordinary* is very far from being confined to Catholics. Indeed I have been puzzled to account for the fact that Catholics, who possess such springs of extraordinary spiritual graces and help, so often make so little use of them in ordinary life, falling behind the standard often set by non-Catholics and even men and women with little religious belief. Hence I for one would welcome as wide a co-operation as possible with all men and women who, whatever their theological position, are in substantial agreement about the need to restore a social order whose ends are the strengthening and maintenance of those spiritual and moral values that have been taught and preserved by Christianity. They may be summarised as justice in an order reflecting God's design and the establishment and cultivation of the conditions for the freedom of the human being to live his life as a being made in the image of God and for a Divine purpose here and hereafter. Or to put it otherwise, the observance of the second commandment "Thou shalt love thy neighbour as thyself" within the order rendered necessary by the observance of the first "Thou shalt love the Lord thy God." As Dorothy Sayers has pointed out, plenty of people seek to observe the second commandment, but with fatal results to society as a whole if they refuse to obey the first—and one might add the remainder that derive from it.

On the other hand the experience of attempts at Christian co-operation, as envisaged in England by the Sword of the Spirit, have led to certain difficulties. Moreover, from the point of view of the argument in these pages, such co-operation tends to strengthen the witness of Christianity as a whole to the *extraordinary* in religious and spiritual life. Bishops of different communions appear on the same platform, speeches revealing the identity of view of Catholics, Anglicans, and others on social questions are made, common programmes embodying Christian principles are worked out. The general effect is to demonstrate that Christians are agreed in principle about many important matters—and there it ends. It reminds one of two acrobats who, having swung down from different ropes, embrace in mid-air and return whence they came. The different communions find themselves in agreement about certain general moral, social, and economic principles, but they agree to differ about the spiritual sources in worship and doctrine of these common views, and, having joined hands about them, they are precluded from seeking to apply them in the only sphere where they can be applied, namely in public and political life. To say this is not to underestimate the value of the progress in co-operation that has been made, but one may ask oneself whether it is ever likely either to work upwards to the springs of this present agreement or outwards to the arena in which the political struggle is fought.

For these reasons it is worth considering whether there is any other form of Christian co-operation which would show greater promise of successful action. I suggest that there is. The trouble about the co-operation so far attempted is that it is co-operation between communions or Churches *as such*. Co-operation between one communion and another must inevitably emphasise the different doctrinal positions of the communions concerned, and consequently lead to considerable awkwardness and instability, as well as practical difficulties that have already been met with in experience. But more important perhaps is the obvious fact that the Church as such is not commissioned to play a political rôle, and must therefore stop short just when the things upon which agreement is possible begin to get interesting, namely in their practical application in political life.

Let me try to make this last point clearer—even though

I have referred to it earlier on—for I am convinced that a consideration of what is involved in it may prove very helpful in this question and in others. A Church is a *religious* institution. Its purpose is to teach men spiritual and moral truths and to provide for them the normal and most secure way of spiritual and moral development in this world and salvation in the next. The Church, to put it in another way, is concerned with the supreme ends of human life and with such means as must necessarily be followed if that end is to be securely attained. That is all. It is not directly concerned with lesser ends, nor with means in general, so long as these lesser ends and means are compatible with the supreme end. The Church teaches me that I have certain duties towards my neighbour; it does not teach me how quickest to ensure that my neighbour enjoys what is due to him. Or again, it teaches me that art and literature and science must be used for God's greater glory and the benefit of God's children; it does not teach me how to paint pictures or write books and conduct scientific experiments which can fulfil this end. And it is the same with politics. The Church insists that the order of society shall be consonant with and helpful towards the pursuit of certain values; it does not teach me that democracy is better than aristocracy or free trade better than protection.

All this is obvious enough. But the next step is not so obvious, or at least not so commonly remembered. Christianity does not claim to be *a* way of salvation here and hereafter. It claims to be *the* way. It claims to speak with the voice of God. This claim implies that the spiritual and moral order taught by the Church is God's pattern for human life and for society. Now though the Church's commission is limited to the supreme ends, and the necessary means to those ends, the *Divine pattern itself is not so limited.* You can say that art or literature or science

or politics, considered in themselves rather than in their
ultimate ends, are outside the Church's domain, but you
cannot say that they are outside God's domain or that their
technique, which depends on truth, is not willed by God.
How then is one to reconcile the limitations of the Church's
commission with the all-embracing nature of the Divine
pattern? *The only answer is that the reconciliation is in the
individual Christian.* In man, God's image, the religious
and the secular are united, whereas the Church is religious
and the State secular. The Christian is a member of the
Church, but he is also a citizen, an artist, a man of business,
a parent, and so on. And the Christianity of the Christian
is not confined to worship or formal doctrine and belief;
it affects every angle and aspect of human life. Though
the Church's field is confined to worship, doctrine, and
moral guidance (the latter comparable to a map with general
direction and routes together with the control of the
traffic lights, "Go" "Wait," "Stop"), the service of God,
in other words the working out of God's pattern, is an
all-time and every-place business for the individual Christian.
He is constantly called upon to make judgments about the
efficiency, suitability, quality, and purpose of his actions and
behaviour, for all these are involved in his duty of seeking
to fit them into the Divine pattern. Religious guidance is
insufficient. It has to be supplemented by training and
education and habit.

Now, if we admit that there is no present solution to
the disunity of worship and doctrine as between different
communions, and if we remember that in fact it is only in
the social, political, and economic spheres—spheres, be it
noted, of citizenship, vocation, and daily life—that there
can be useful Christian co-operation, surely we should look
for a field of co-operation where in fact the practical work
of civics and business is carried out. In other words, we
should look to the world and not to the Church as such.

The objection to this—or rather perhaps the slowness of people to see this—is simply due to the entirely erroneous idea that there is a distinction between the world and Christianity in the same way as there is a valid distinction between the world or State and the Church. For the Christian there is no such distinction. The God revealed in his religion is the God of the world.

What form then should such co-operation take? I suggest that it should be co-operation between individual Christian persons *in their quality of citizens who are Christians*. And this is political co-operation to defend and promote in the field of politics (in the broadest sense) the moral, social, and economic principles taught by Christianity.

Before further describing the nature and possibilities of such political Christian co-operation, let me point out the novelty of the idea at the present time. In all the proposals and movements put forward under Christian auspices for the restoration of a Christian order it is always (so far as I am aware) a question of the Church or the Churches. Christianity in fact is identified, among Christians as well as others, with the ecclesiastical institution and its clerical leaders. The State to all intents and purposes only recognises the existence of Christianity in an institution personified in its highest dignitaries. For all it cares, the Church might just as well be a sect. The clergy, with the laity in their wake, are always closely associated with Christian action, secular as well as ecclesiastical. (All this is natural and in a sense correct. I am not suggesting that Christians are half inside and half outside the Church. They are wholly members of the Church and it is as members of the Church—the Church, not *a* Church or sect—that they are Christians. But it still remains a fact that many of their activities are outside the direct authority of the Church and only negatively affected—*ratione peccati*, as the theologians put it—by the Church's indirect authority.

Yet these secular activities too are Christian, and indeed it may be contended that to-day they are the most important Christian activities so far as the world is concerned. The overlooking of this, both within and outside the Church, is extremely significant.)

The nature of the political Christian co-operation which I have in mind must vary according to the circumstances of different countries and according to the times. Thus in this country at any rate anything in the nature of a Christian political party would be out of place. (I would contend, in fact, that a Christian political party is a self-contradictory notion, for every political party should be open to every citizen, but a Christian party of its nature must exclude all whose conscience would not permit them to co-operate with Christians.) But there is nothing to prevent the formation of a lay political Christian union charged with the defence of Christian moral and social principles and the promotion of Christian values in central and local government, through the creation of a public opinion in the matter by speech and writing, and by its own study and action towards the formulation of an ever clearer and more defined policy. Such methods as the questioning of political candidates for Parliament and local authorities, the drawing up of manifestos and petitions in the name of the great numbers that might be expected to join a properly organised movement, the holding of public meetings, central action in the capital or big cities and localised action in every part of the country—these surely would not be without a notable effect on the country as a whole. In fact they would be the public representation of the Christian convictions of perhaps ten million people who have hitherto found themselves publicly represented as far as all other important aspects of their civic life are concerned, but never in so far as their Christian values are.

Such a movement would not interfere with normal

political allegiances. There is nothing to prevent Christians from belonging to different political parties, economic and industrial associations, professional societies, and so on. But within each of these is much room indeed for the clarification of ends according to Christian ideas. "Labour" may well believe that a considerable and rapid socialisation is the best technical means of organising the country and the surest safeguard of human rights, while Tories may disagree. Different Christians, conscientiously following their consciences and seeking to use the light of the reason God gave them in terms of their experience, may be Conservative, Liberal, or Labour. But whatever their views as to means, there is room for common action about ends, as well as common action to prevent the pursuit of disordered ends and immoral means. There is Christian work to do within each party and association, and work that can be done in conjunction with members of other parties without the slightest disloyalty to one's own. And there are occasions (increasingly frequent) when common Christian action outside party is imperative.

This then would be a kind of Christian co-operation that would be far more effective than present attempts to co-operate within Churches or communions, debarred as these are from political action and consequently of too little interest in their field to the Christian citizen. Starting as it would from the political end, that is from ordinary daily life—in which in any case Christians find themselves often co-operating—emphasis on doctrinal differences would be at its minimum. But there would be good hope that this common Christian action by citizens exercising their normal civic functions would lead gradually to a greater understanding and agreement, and these could not be without their good effect on differences about worship and faith.

To end on the most practical note, I envisage a kind of lay Council of Action of perhaps some hundred members, drawn from political, business, professional, art, artisan, and worker circles, with an executive committee. This central council would be linked with provincial councils of the same character in the big cities and local councils in as many townships and villages as possible. There would be no attempt to elect or co-opt according to denomination (still less spiritual reputation) but, among those who can accept a Christian constitution in public affairs, solely according to ability, interest, power, or leadership.

(vi) THE EFFECT OF INTERNATIONAL CHRISTIAN ACTION (SECULAR AS WELL AS RELIGIOUS) ON THE WORLD

The international benefits that must accrue from a Christian organisation, beginning with a fuller sense of the necessity of Christianity in daily life within the different communions and spreading to a wider co-operation through the activities of citizens as Christians, an organisation at work within the world and representative of intelligently led and responsible Christians with personal initiative in temporal affairs, needs no stressing. The trouble about Christian principles on war and peace, on social justice, on human liberty is that they are generally taken as irrelevant to world conditions as they are, however desirable they may be considered to be in an ideal world. But in the last analysis they are irrelevant only because those who are prepared to act in accordance with them constitute the tiniest minority of people, so strange to the world that they are thought to be cranks. Is not the instinct of the devout Catholic, of the priest, of the contemplative religious himself, to see how far the Pope, for example, can be said to support the national cause or the present order? But if the very substantial number of Catholics, let alone other Christians, in every country were trained to think of Papal pronouncements, especially those addressed to the whole world, as common principles to be applied to the particular conditions of each nation, instead of the other way round, the present gulf between the ideal and the practical would already be bridged.   I am not over-sanguine in this matter. I do not envisage any possible quick solution.   Even the general acceptance of the Pope's lead would not solve the technical difficulties of practical application nor prevent foolish, cranky, and impossible interpretations.   None the less it has become ever more clear in recent history that disorder and war have resulted from the failure of the nations, with their increasingly totalitarian regimes, to find common ground between them.   The search for this common ground and the evidence of the need for it are to be found in the rise of the great ideologies, but since these ideologies are particularist in their source, being based either on nationalism itself or upon a class distinction, these new religions only increase the tension.   And even if one of them were to triumph after the War, the resulting unity would be artificial, unstable, and to be maintained only by force.   In contrast to these stands the balanced, sober, "platitudinous" common sense of a Christian order that is based upon the order, balance, and harmony of the human person, reflecting the Divine Nature itself.   That order, being concerned with spiritual and moral values, can be inserted as a leaven into most human political and economic systems, and these will in fact tend to approximate to one another, in so far as Christians succeed in inserting that Christian leaven.   That Christians themselves should betray this ideal, preferring the particularism of national, economic, and social divisions, is difficult to understand except in the light of an almost total loss of the sense of Christian unity outside an arbitrarily cut-off religious field.

The restoration of this international Christian order, which in many of its most important functions could cover non-Catholic Christianity, is so necessary, and so obviously implied in Christianity itself, that one feels that the mere creation of a new machinery by leaders who realise the point would suffice to bring it about again. And once brought about the actual history of Western civilisation must take a different turn. Things have been allowed to go too far for any quick or easy solution, and, in any case, the mistakes of the past will have to be paid for in full, but a living autonomous and flexible Catholic and Christian international organisation transcending the ecclesiastical field, and supporting an active Christian sense of the relation between spiritual and temporal, would at least ensure the fact that the future would be a slow climb again towards sanity and not a desperate recourse to yet further insanities to cure insanity.

Taking then all these suggestions together we can obtain the vision of a Catholicity spiritual and secular, trained in the home and the schools (if possible), maintained and strengthened in the parish, and at work in and through the national life by means of such a lay and independent, yet fully instructed and wisely guided, loose-knit organisation for the purposes of intelligent and effective action—the whole balancing, as it were, the already admirable and essentially unchanging spiritual hierarchy, organisation, and sacramental life. One sees too the possibility of Christian civic action united and organised among a wide range of Christian men and women, unhappily still divided as to communion.

One realises, of course, that any such plan can only be developed in the course of years, and that conditions for its growth become almost daily less favourable. Yet some such ideal must surely be held up before us, so that we may all the time be adapting it to what may be possible here and now in this or that country. It is the way of a clever world to try by every means to throw us back into our spiritual catacombs where we can do little harm. But the original catacombs were not catacombs in that sense. Despite them—indeed their importance has been widely exaggerated—the fully balanced Catholic life was being lived, and the Christians were carrying it into practice all the time. Whatever the conditions it is always possible to keep alive this double functioning of spiritual and secular within the one uniform pattern. The tragedy is that we only begin to see the need clearly when the chances of fully expressing it are rapidly retreating.

CHAPTER VI

A NEW PENTECOST

(i) THE REAL DANGER WILL BE IN FALSE CONSTRUCTION
AFTER THE WAR

IT is time we gathered together the threads of the argument which our survey has suggested.

My central position is this. I am utterly convinced that the complete solution to the perplexities of the contemporary world is to be found in the Catholic Church, the full expression of a Christianity which overflows its own visible frontiers. I also believe that a distressed world, yet a generous and often noble world of men and women with qualities no less fine than in any previous generation, would welcome the Church if it knew and understood it. Yet the world and organised Christianity stand apart from one another for important reasons which have not been sufficiently studied on either side.

The world, as I see it, is in danger of becoming even more deeply bogged in error. Its very struggle to save itself—a struggle of men and women prepared for amazing self-sacrifice and intense devotion to what they believe to be right but is in fact often deeply wrong, and generally disorientated—carries it ever deeper into the waste and mire and darkness. Though the fury of this world-struggle must end some time, I cannot see how cessation of war by itself can save us. In the first place, I do not see how the world in its present economic position, and torn by ideological rivalries and the fight for an economic well-being consonant with the expectations engendered by education and the progress of science and technology, can at present accept the principles of peace and a new order laid down again and again by the Pope and echoed by Christian leaders. Those principles imply a yet longer and more painful struggle, the struggle against the false values which men in general still worship. The Papal principles, I suggest—and I do it, I believe, on the authority of the Pope himself— will only become practical when men are prepared to submit their passions, their claims, their very wants to a prior necessity: the necessity for a common recognition of a universal norm of morality founded in God's own Revelation—a Revelation, through the Church, through the Christian tradition, and through the human reason, of God's own design or pattern for human life and life of human society. It may be that many—more than we suppose— are prepared individually for this task. They may not understand the matter in those terms, but substantially they realise the need for an order, international and national, directed towards affording to all human beings the liberty, cultural and economic, which will enable them to live up to the highest that they know to be in them. And even though they may not see the order within which alone that liberty can be secured, they would welcome it if they saw it. I cannot believe that men and women ready to accept with gladness the sacrifices and hardships of a prolonged war fought for an ideology, *i.e.* a faith greater than themselves, are not also ready to sacrifice themselves to this higher ideal if once they understood it. In this readiness to sacrifice and in this fundamental seriousness of purpose lies the material for a happier future. Here is the stuff which the Papal programmes can one day "inform." Here is something to be getting on with—to put it crudely.

But the immediate practical problem seems to be of a different character. At the present time all this potential goodness is imprisoned. It is imprisoned in artificial groups, in false ideals, in the very technique of a totalitarian or semi-totalitarian political and economic life. Above all it is imprisoned in war, which, as the Pope has reminded us again and again, makes matters progressively worse, the longer it endures.

I cannot see any hope of a sufficient release from these constraints unless it be in too sudden and too complete a release through a post-War political and economic collapse. Such a collapse of a highly specialised and highly centralised world, whose members have come to rely so completely on nationally controlled order and internationally controlled economic relations, would be even worse than the present false orders. The best practical hope, as I have said, would seem to lie in the temporary assumption of a large measure of control by victor countries working in with the best elements in neutral and ex-enemy countries. But my fear in this case is lest the progressive, materialist, human-beatitude-on-earth-for-all philosophy, which has sought to express itself in the past in the cult of socialism or fascism, should become the sole popular drive or urge behind the great social and economic Machine or Machines that will inevitably be set up. This popular drive for security and pleasure will be utilised by economic and industrial forces to complete the creation of the planned Machine State, whose end tends to be its own productive efficiency quite irrespective of the spiritual, moral, and cultural good of those who are obliged to work it, and who receive in compensation mass-comfort, mass-culture and mass-dope. And we must remember that, given the immense mind-conditioning powers of the modern mechanised propaganda, this solution will be sincerely welcomed by very many people,

In this lies the greatest danger. It is not the danger of the War itself, since war, whatever its horrors and falsities, cannot in itself be constructive. War is but the break-up of what was rotten in the past. When things reach a certain stage it may even be the only bridge from the past into a different future. It is on the shape of that future that all depends. Yet to-day, in the clash of false ideologies, we must be prepared for a new constructive era which will mark the triumph of an ideology that is anti-Christian. For the fact is that the conflicting ideologies bear a considerable and increasing resemblance to one another, and they are all the effect, under different historic and national conditions, of man's struggle to find a materialistic solution to the technical and economic problems set by materialistic progress.

I do not forget the clean-cut difference between the cause of the Allies, who defend what we call the decencies of civilised life, and the cause of the enemy, who has no scruple in flouting every law of man and God in his attempt to destroy the old and create the new. But if we dig deeper we shall reach even more fundamental issues. We shall understand the great struggle between rival factions, rival interests, rival traditions to dominate the totalitarian machine which alone can control a world of intense economic and technological complexity inhabited by men and women moulded by contemporary materialist education, and intent on sharing the same desires and aspirations for security, comfort, and pleasure. The tragedy of the times lies in the almost universal prostitution of the higher powers of man, who is spirit as well as animal, in the service of this ideal, which he himself can easily confound with genuine moral values in patriotism, international idealism and nobility of nationalism, co-operation and justice, freedom, a new order.

In Christianity alone, which rescued, preserved, and raised these true values, lies the solution, but at the moment there is no real relationship, no real connection, between the warring, changing world and the Christian order.

(ii) THREE REASONS WHY CHRISTIANITY IS NOT ASKED TO HELP

There is no connection for a great many reasons.

In the first place, Christianity can offer no clear-cut, practical solution to the world's technical problems. The Church teaches the spiritual, moral, and temporal values that should be striven for; it warns against false ways; above all it canalises God's grace so that souls may be rescued from what would otherwise appear to be a spiritual hopelessness. And if men or a society of men are Christian, that man or that society of men will gradually work its way to a temporal order that is compatible with Christianity. But the spiritual conversion must come first and it must be maintained over a long period. Yet the world is in such chaos that it insistently calls for immediate, practical help. It must find a way out or perish in anarchy. In that sense there is no Christian way out. The technical temporal problems of politics and economics must be solved in their own order, just as the engineer must solve the technical problems set him in the construction of a bridge or a dam.[1] In the temporal order the Church can warn men of what

[1] The Beveridge Social Insurance Plan seems to me an excellent example of the facing of a technical problem and seeking a solution in terms of the practicable. It is non-party and non-ideological, and as such it appears to be entirely consistent with Christian ends. It demands only to be applied with Christian motives and charity and in a Christian setting.

is wrong; it can guide them so that they may work in the right direction; with its long experience of men and affairs it can even give invaluable hints in their own business (as the Pope is doing); but the practical problems are the world's own business. All that can be said is that their solution will be made much easier if nations and men attend to the Church's warnings and advice and if they endeavour to live their temporal and spiritual lives by the same supernatural ideals.

But this consideration, which is not sufficiently understood, undoubtedly acts as a deterrent. Men who realise it shrug their shoulders and say that the Church can only offer platitudes for advice. Men who turn with earnestness towards Christianity feel let down because the Church cannot tell them what exactly to do in order to overcome their puzzles.

In the second place, man to-day is so steeped in false ideals that there appears to be no relation between *his* goodness and the goodness which Christianity proposes. Heroism, self-sacrifice, charity, devotion, all of them often exercised to the degree reached in the annals of the martyrs, are stimulated by temporal ends, such as the fight for a new social order or the maintenance of an imperilled old one. And with the loss of a real faith in God, and an objective moral norm, these temporal causes become a substitute for religion. They are worshipped for their own sake. It is true that the frightful consequences of that worship are beginning to make themselves felt, and men are wondering. Few reflecting people can accept the terrible prostitution of so much good for so much evil. Few can fail to discern how good and contrary good, how good and evil, are inextricably confused in the causes for which men lay down their lives and all that makes life worth living. But an abyss still divides those who are so wondering from the only faith strong and deep enough to rescue them from the despair which disillusion must otherwise bring.   That faith is faith in God; God, not a name for labelling their own personal desires and ideals, but the Supreme objectively existing Reality Whose pattern for human life has been revealed in history, Who took flesh so that *the* concrete example of human thinking and living might be given us, Who is still with us in the Sacrament of the Altar and the Mystical Body, at once providing the grace for personal salvation and endowing with vitality the Church and body of Christians, as well as all who seek to follow their consciences, that not the individual alone but society itself may become reordered according to the Divine design.

And this brings us to the third reason for the lack of contact between world and Church, the failure of Christians to carry their secret—a secret long lost to the world as such —into the market-place.

Faith in God and faith in God's Church have been lost. We need not inquire into the reasons; the fact is plain. Too many Christians themselves cannot to-day be said so much to possess their faith as to cling on to a remnant of it. *They hope in God for another world; they are losing their faith in God as a factor of supreme importance for this one.*   Their daily life is lived in accordance with the gospel of the day in a slightly bowdlerised edition.   They turn away from certain grosser passages which scandalise them, but they accept that gospel as a whole.   And if some still fight shy of the whole plain meaning, they can easily be taken through line by line and persuaded that each line, taken by itself—apart from the above-mentioned grosser ones which are not stressed in the lesson—is allowable.

This is a poor sort of introduction of the Church into the world.   I am not talking of virtue or vice.   It would be well, of course, if all Catholics were models of virtue, though I doubt if the world expects that.   Indeed one of the strongest natural attractions of the Church is the gaiety and *insouciance* of its members. The Catholic sense of dependence on God's mercy, the Catholic refusal to despair because of falls and sins, the work of the confessional— these in the long run are assets in a world which takes itself so seriously. I am talking of a spiritual and moral indifference to the problems, national, social, economic, political, which are breaking men's lives. It is not in the clear-cut difference between right and wrong, virtue and vice, a good life and a self-indulgent one that the trouble to-day for the most part arises; it is in the debated and crucial field where right fights with right, where one ideal destroys another, where goodness in trying to serve good produces evil, where the claims of society infringe the rights of men, where one code seems correct for the nation and another for the individual. Yet it is here that the average Christian appears least interested, and most easily content to accept the dominating force of the moment.

And it does not seem as though the attempt on the part of the minority to follow a path of higher perfection lessens the evil. For in this case the temptation is not to mingle with the world and share its philosophy but to turn one's back upon it altogether, to indulge in a sort of "quietism," as though to the holy soul the lower order did not matter. Certainly the world is in general edified by the virtue and holiness of men and women who demonstrate such faith in their religion that the world ceases to mean very much to them. Here the world finds the evidence it needs of a Christian sincerity and toughness all too rare in nominally Christian circles. Many individuals may indeed be so impressed as to inquire further, and perhaps one day be set themselves along the way to God. But for the most part this holiness in retreat from the world becomes an occasion of admiration rather than imitation and comfort.

(iii) THE LANGUAGE OF CHRISTIANITY IN THE MARKET-PLACE

How then can this abyss between world and Church be crossed?

It is vain, I think, to comfort ourselves with empty and unreal hopes. We must recognise—and the world must recognise—that Christianity of itself cannot solve all problems. The Church is a religious institution. It professes to link man and society with God, not to create a perfect temporal society. Its action on temporal society can only be indirect, and the effectiveness of that action depends not so much on the Church as such, as on the individual Christians who in their persons and lives link the spiritual and the temporal orders. Temporal welfare and order are possible consequences of true religious profession, not a necessary characteristic of it. We shall surely all go astray if we do not recognise that the Church can only *directly* offer supernatural salvation *out* of a disordered world. But the way to that salvation ought not to be through a magic word unlocking a secret in a separated room. That salvation is meant to be through the ordering of *all* that is disordered, and therefore it ought of its nature to help towards temporal order. And the good effects it leaves in its wake are not confined to those who have trodden the true path; they help everyone. That is why in a Christianly ordered society those who may not share the faith can still benefit from it and be inspired by it. That is why in our own times, and in those which have preceded them, so much good has been done by non-Christians who have shared in the broad Christian inheritance of an earlier age.

But as Catholics we can never really hope to avoid the central issue: the issue of conversion. The world must regain its faith if Christian salvation is to shed its indirect ordering blessings upon it. But so long as that faith remains hidden, turned away, incomprehensible, concerned only with the non-temporal, how shall the world discover it and fit itself to receive the grace needed to recover it?

It must be expressed in the only language which the world to-day understands, in actions which—if I may so put it—are worthy of a world which, with all its weaknesses, is seeking for a better order and dying for it. That is the language of the market-place, the language of politics and economics and social affairs and war and peace and education and art and recreation and the vexations and troubles of daily life. Those actions must be actions on the same plane as the actions of the leaders of rival ideologies and their fanatical servants, on the same plane as the actions of those who suffer and die for what is left of their beliefs and ideals.

All this, I repeat, cannot be the business of the Church as such. We are leaving the sphere of the spiritual and even the sphere of the direct relation of the spiritual to the temporal. The Church which stands for all and lays down, in God's name, that which is essential to all and is universally valid cannot fully direct each individual member in his or her daily life and decisions. The Church guides and inspires, but what should we think of any other society whose members confined themselves to doing the least possible, or who carefully separated from their daily works and avocations the guiding inspiration of the society's ideals?

It is upon ourselves that falls the duty of carrying Christian inspiration, Christian light, Christian order into the midst of a world of which we are full citizens. And if the world could distinguish a Christian by his *difference*, by his expression in political, social, and business life of a faith in values that are in opposition to what the world is seeking, than this example of the "extraordinary" in ordinary life would arrest its attention and draw it into a closer inquiry into the sources of that "extraordinary" behaviour. Then the "extraordinary" of the Faith itself, hitherto felt to be obscurantism or magic or medieval superstition, would appear as the compelling source of action which truly edifies and helps the world.

That, let us recall, was the mode of action of the early Christians, whose situation resembles our own so closely in many ways, as the Holy Father has lately reminded us. These early Christians stood out. They stood out indeed by their piety and their mysteries; but to the world they stood out most by their attitude to what was taken for granted. There was no attempt to seek political separation, no attempt to evade the full duties of citizenship, no attempt to escape; yet the very refusal to accept the false conventions founded in pagan ideals—even though a casuist might have worked out some acceptable formula—caught the attention of the Empire and in the end conquered it. These early Christians did not wait for orders; they did not expect the Church as such to lay down authoritative moral decisions. It was they who, inspired with the example of Christ and strengthened with His spirit, set the pace and created a new living society.

(iv) A STRUGGLE AGAINST THE STREAM

The shape of the new world to come after the War, and even during the War, cannot be foretold. For Christians it may be a time of persecution, of ever-increasing State despotism, of intolerable political conditions. It is not merely fanciful to say that if God allows such times to come for all of us it may be for our good. For the Christian is at his best under conditions of persecution when the tyrant himself clarifies the issues. Then the Christian has no option but to give up or live up to the extraordinary in the faith. And it is always that extraordinary which impresses itself upon the world and in the end conquers.

It is perhaps more likely that the new era will deal more subtly with Christianity. It will grant it relative liberty— liberty to worship, liberty even to maintain its apostolic work within set limits, liberty perhaps to make dignified and safe protests. But the granting of such liberty will be made dependent upon an unwritten bargain, a bargain that the Church will remain loyal to Cæsar, that the Church will help Cæsar whenever it possibly can, that the Church will never make itself a serious nuisance and that it will come down upon any of its faithful who show signs of breaking the bond. That is the supremely dangerous condition for the Church. That is the condition which makes it hard indeed for the Church to affect the world and for the world to understand the Church, for the Church is turned into an uninteresting and servile sect.

Whatever happens, Christians must train themselves in order to preserve their real liberties, the liberty of conscience which allows and encourages the Christian to be fully a Christian in the whole of his life, no matter how much he may be mocked by the world—and by some of his fellow-Christians; the liberty to teach and pass on that message of freedom and courage even though it be only through a look of encouragement in a concentration camp; the liberty to speak one's mind fully, even though it be in a secretly published paper or on the scaffold itself. We do not look to the State for these liberties, for the State cannot deprive us of them. For these we have to look to ourselves, to our fellow-Christians, to our own superiors, to the inspiration and education which they are giving and will give to those who come after us.

Must we always wait for persecution to come in all its force in order to confess the fullness of our faith as it

5*

affects our lives as a whole and lives of all our fellow-men? Must we always fall victims to the cleverness of the world's leaders who fear us and know so well how to tame us?

We remain—or try to remain—loyal to our faith: many live lives filled with goodness and holiness. But the world around us to-day is a witness to the insufficiency of this. We live in a time of crisis. We live in a time which is shaping a mysterious and unforeseeable future. A heritage of disbelief, of false values, of complex and ill-understood progress in material achievement, is working itself out through clash and suffering, either to a climax of a victorious materialistic order or to a long period of anarchy and confusion. The fine emotions in mankind, the idealism, the courage, the capacity for sacrifice—all so wonderfully exemplified in this country at war, both in its profession of moral faith and in the way in which it endures—are already being utilised by the great economic Machine in its unconscious purpose to use men as pleasure-doped and comfort-doped *things* which serve it, and they will be utilised still further unless the Machine is crushed under its own weight in this gigantic struggle for mastery. And yet there is offered to men the means of escape, the know-ledge of the principles upon which a new order could be built. But something is wanted. It is faith, a faith that can move men to those particular sacrifices—no more difficult than the ones they gladly accept to-day—which these principles demand, a faith that can cause men to *believe* the simple truth which their hearts and their common sense already offer them. This Christianity is too easy by half, they say in one breath. It is far too hard and absurd and paradoxical and antiquated, they say in the next. But it is *not* easy to live by Christian principles in a non-Christian world which sets store on so much that can have little meaning in the true Christian. Few Christians attempt it. They evade the difficulty. They lead their Christian life along safe, if often hard, paths; but they suspend it when they find themselves in the broad flow of temporal non-Christian life. They console themselves with the thought that they can reach a Christian bank and rest whenever they feel inclined or compelled. They forget however that unless they fight against the stream itself they reach every time a different point along the bank, a point further down-stream and one less secure. The world wants to see the struggle against the stream, not the drift and the rescue. It wants to see what strength this vaunted force of Christianity can give a man. And if it sees the struggle, it will once again seek out the source of the strength which Christians imbibe in their strange mysteries, in their rigid dogmas, in their unyielding moral teaching.

(v) THE LINK BETWEEN CHURCH AND WORLD IS THE INDIVIDUAL CHRISTIAN DE-MONSTRATING CHRIST

And when the world sees Christianity in action, in the battlefield of daily life, not just formulated in abstractions or practised in safe retreats and on a chosen soil against what seems to it like a shadow army, it will learn the truth. It will learn that Christianity offers the world not quack remedies, no easy way out, but only an unshakable, virile faith in God, Whose pattern has been revealed to men. The task of shaping the world to that pattern never ceases, success is never achieved—yet all the time progress can be made and victories can be won. Gradually, slowly, the design appears, the effect of men and more men labouring at their temporal works under the light of the Holy Spirit. As that faith is regained, so will the vicissitudes of worldly business count far less in the certainty of an end that *can* be reached; and as that faith is regained, so imperceptibly is order being restored until men come to find again *the* order, which reflects God's own design.

The future of a torn world does not depend upon any Pope, who as Vicar of Christ preserves God's revelation and teaches in His name, and who guides and helps the world with the experience of two thousand years of human history behind him; it does not depend upon any Bishop, who, as the successor of the Apostles, also rules and teaches the flock of the fold entrusted to him; it does not depend upon any preacher or teacher or writer who may weave ingenious theories of social and political reform; the future of a torn world depends, under God, upon the apostolic life and example of the Christian as Christian, standing in the market-place, and by his daily habit of life in mind, will, and character seeking, within his own limits and opportunities, to complete Christ's own work—a work which the limits of time and space rendered it impossible for the Incarnate God to perform. For to each Christian there is set the ideal of being "another Christ" in those unique circumstances of time and space within which his particular life runs. Each Christian, as a member of Christ's Mystical Body, jointly with his fellow-Christians, in full submission to the authority and teaching of Christ through His Church, is called upon to make each thought and act of his an example of Christian truth over against the values which the world may profess.

There and there alone is to be found the link, many millions of times repeated, between the Church and the world. There and there alone is, under God Himself, the hope of a world order after the design which God has revealed.

I cannot see that anything less than this de-*monstration* of the concrete application of Christian truth to temporal problems is involved in the Gospels, the teaching of the Church, and the Pope's great messages to the modern world. What the Pope has had to say in his allocutions directly related to the warring world springs directly from

the balanced principles of Christian action, as they should
be expressed in the moral outlook of the majority of
Christians in their own personal and civic life.

(vi) THE GIFT OF TONGUES WITH WHICH TO SPEAK TO THE WORLD

For a predominantly non-believing world my conclusion
—if true—would seem to be a despairing one, for we must
admit that there is no immediate prospect of the acceptance
by the world of the "mysteries" of the Christian faith, nor
a great prospect of Christians themselves de-monstrating
Christ in the market-place. But Christianity, though its
dogma, sacraments, and moral intransigence seem strange
to a world without supernatural faith, is not a peculiar or
esoteric cult. Its outward expression and behaviour are in
fact nothing but ordered and harmonised common sense,
nothing but those maxims which the world instinctively
calls "platitudes," so obvious is their truth once they are
expressed. It is the distance between ordinary life as it
is, with its selfishness, its apparent conflicts of duty, its
confused issues, its clash between good and good and good
and bad, on one side, and, on the other, the common-sense
Christian order of friendship, charity, justice, the sub-
ordination of the lesser end to the higher that is bridged
by the "mysteries," the "extraordinary" in the Faith.

If Christians themselves, who live and believe these
"mysteries" of faith in God, of revelation, of spiritual and
sacramental life, do not in consequence express in their own
social lives the very order which is so lost to the world
that it seems to it both a platitude and an unattainable ideal,
how can we expect the world to recover faith in a cause
of which there are so few visible effects? On the other
hand, if Christians themselves demonstrated the effects of
the cause in which they have faith, they themselves in the

first place would be surprised to see their own Faith quicken and strengthen and perhaps lead to greater unity between themselves; the world would next be startled to find *the* ideal realised; in the third place, the world would see that this ideal was a platitude come, as it were, to life and therefore easily lived; and lastly, it would then at least interest itself again in the cause of a miracle so extraordinary in its happening and yet so simple and homely in its results.

With some hundreds of millions of Catholics and other Christians in the world, is all this so wholly impracticable? That all Christians, still less all men, should become saints is most unlikely. But I confess that I cannot see any good reason why a sufficient number of Christians should not be trained to possess Christian minds, Christian eyes, Christian ears, and Christian tongues. Being human, they will abuse them all more or less, but at present they can only rarely—even though their souls be Christian—be said even to possess these means of maintaining Christian relations with the world around them.

Two thousand years ago "the multitude came together and were confounded in mind because that every man heard them speak in his own tongue. And they were all amazed and wondered, saying: Behold are not all these that speak Galilean? And how have we heard every man our own tongue wherein we were born?" And would not our present world, with its troubles and vexations and disappointments, yet withal with its goodness, its idealism, its search for something in keeping with the dignity of man, be once again confounded if Christians spoke Christianity again in the language of the market-place, of the parliaments, of the chancelleries, of the stock exchanges, of the factories, of the farms, so that every man could hear in his own tongue? Would it not then discover that its perplexing technical, social, and economic problems yielded more easily to the spirit of man when it truly seeks to use creatures for ends commensurate with human dignity, instead of being content to remain the instrument of a sub-human purpose.

"And all they that believed were together and had all things common. Their possessions and goods they sold, and divided them to all, according as every one had need. And continuing daily with one accord in the temple, and breaking bread from house to house, they took their meat with gladness and simplicity of heart, praising God and having favour with all the people. And the Lord increased daily together such as should be saved."

Jm 160